Walking
with the
Apostles

Forty-Five Days
in the
Book of Acts

Denzil R. Miller

Walking with the Apostles: Forty-Five Days in the Book of Acts.
© 2016 Denzil R. Miller. All rights reserved. No part of this publication may be reproduced, distributed, or transmitted in any form or by any means, including photocopying, recording, or other electronic or mechanical methods, without the prior written permission of the copyright holder, except in the case of brief quotations embodied in critical reviews and certain other noncommercial uses permitted by copyright law.

Unless otherwise noted, Scripture quotations are from the HOLY BIBLE, NEW INTERNATIONAL VERSION®. NIV®. Copyright © 1973, 1978, 1984 by International Bible Society. Used by permission of Zondervan. All rights reserved worldwide.

Biblical quotations marked NKJV are taken from the New King James Version. Copyright © 1982 by Thomas Nelson, Inc. Used by permission. All rights reserved.

Biblical quotations marked NASB are taken from the New American Standard Bible® Copyright © 1960, 1962, 1963, 1968, 1971, 1972, 1973, 1975, 1977, 1995 by The Lockman Foundation. Used by permission.

Miller, Denzil R., 1946—
www.DenzilRMiller.com
Walking with the Apostles: Forty-Five Days in the Book of Acts.
/ Denzil R. Miller.

1. Biblical studies—Acts   2. Pneumatology—Lukan—Pentecostal
3. Missions—Strategy.   4. Theology—Pastoral

ISBN: 978-0-9971750-0-4

PneumaLife Publications
3766 N. Delaware Ave.
Springfield, MO 65803
2016

Printed in the United States of America

Contents

Introduction 1
Day 1: Introducing Acts 5
Day 2: Jesus Promises the Spirit 11
Day 3: Pentecost: The Spirit is Poured Out 17
Day 4: Pentecost: Peter's Spirit-Inspired Message 23
Day 5: More Lessons from Pentecost 29
Day 6: A New Prophetic Community 35
Day 7: Miracle at the Beautiful Gate 41
Day 8: Bold Witness Before the Jewish Leaders 47
Day 9: A Second Outpouring in Jerusalem 53
Day 10: A Conspiracy is Unmasked 59
Day 11: Continued Witness in Jerusalem 65
Day 12: A Spirit-Guided Decision 69
Day 13: Stephen's Spirit-Empowered Witness and Death 73
Day 14: Philip's Powerful Ministry in Samaria 77
Day 15: The Samaritan Outpouring 81
Day 16: Philip's Spirit-Directed Ministry in Gaza 87
Day 17: Saul Meets Jesus 91
Day 18: Saul is Empowered by the Holy Spirit 95
Day 19: Peter Ministers in Judea 101
Day 20: The Holy Spirit Is Poured Out on the Gentiles 107
Day 21: A Missionary Church is Born 113
Day 22: Persecution, Prayer, and Deliverance 119

Day 23: The Gentile Mission is Launched 125
Day 24: Spirit-Empowered Ministry on Cyprus 131
Day 25: The Gospel is Proclaimed in Pisidian Antioch 137
Day 26: Miracles in Iconium, Lystra and Derbe 143
Day 27: Missionary Council in Jerusalem 149
Day 28: Paul's Second Journey Begins 155
Day 29: The Spirit Guides the Missionaries 161
Day 30: The Gospel Goes to Europe 165
Day 31: Imprisonment and Deliverance in Philippi 169
Day 32: Ministry in Thessalonica and Berea 173
Day 33: Paul Preaches in Athens 177
Day 34: Successful Ministry in Corinth 183
Day 35: The Ephesian Outpouring 189
Day 36: The New Testament Strategy of the Spirit 195
Day 37: A Final Farewell 201
Day 38: To Jerusalem: Journey, Arrival, and Arrest 207
Day 39: Trials in Jerusalem 213
Day 40: Paul's Trials before Felix and Festus 219
Day 41: Paul's Trial before Agrippa 225
Day 42: Perilous Journey to Rome 229
Day 43: Miraculous Ministry on Malta 235
Day 44: Paul Preaches in Rome 239
Day 45: The Message of Acts 245
Other Books by Denzil R. Miller 251

Jesus' Last Words:

*"But you will receive power
when the Holy Spirit comes on you;
and you will be my witnesses in Jerusalem,
and in all Judea and Samaria,
and to the ends of the earth."*

~ Acts 1:8 ~

Introduction

The year was 1909. The place was the coastal city of Valparaiso, Chile. The members of the First Methodist Church had gathered for their weekly Sunday school class. Their pastor, Dr. Willis Hoover, was teaching from the Book of Acts. One of the members asked him, "Pastor, what prevents our being a church like the Early Church?"

"Nothing," Dr. Hoover answered, "except something within ourselves." Thus challenged, the congregation started praying for an outpouring of the Spirit upon their church and upon their country. Soon a revival began, with hundreds of church members being baptized in the Holy Spirit. As the newly Spirit-filled members went out and told their friends about Christ, the church began to grow as never before.

Today, the Pentecostal Methodist Church, which sprang from that revival, is the largest Protestant denomination in Chile, with more than 3,000 congregations and 1.5 million members. One local church, the Jotabeche Pentecostal Methodist Church, boasts more than 350,000 members. There are almost two million Pentecostals in Chile, amounting to 15 percent of the total population.

The Chilean revival is but one example of what has occurred all over the world in the past century. Since its inception, the modern Pentecostal Movement has soared from a handful of adherents to about 750 million worldwide. More than a million local congregations can trace their roots to the revival. It is possibly the most studied religious movement in the world today.

What accounts for this amazing growth? There are, of course, many factors. One major factor is, what could be called, the Pentecostal "theology of empowerment." Pentecostal's believe that any follower of Christ, no matter how poor or marginalized, can be supernaturally empowered by the Holy Spirit. Because of this, they can fully and effectively participate in God's mission to redeem the nations.

Pentecostals further believe that this divine empowerment comes as a result of one's being baptized in the Holy Spirit as portrayed in the Book of Acts. They generally describe the experience as being separate from the new birth and accompanied by Spirit-inspired speaking in tongues. Its primary purpose is to empower believers as Christ's witnesses to the lost. This theology of empowerment has emboldened Pentecostals to attempt the seemingly impossible.

The thing that *theologically* distinguishes Pentecostalism from the rest of Evangelical Christianity is how each approaches the Book of Acts. Non-Pentecostals typically read Acts as a book of sacred history. Pentecostals, however, read it as a present-day model of how the church ought to carry out its mission. They see the Book of Acts as a divinely inspired missions manual describing how believers can be Christ's Spirit-empowered witnesses "in Jerusalem, and in all Judea and Samaria, and to the ends of the earth."

Pentecostals therefore closely identify with the apostles and other Spirit-filled disciples in Acts. They reason: if they ministered in power, so should we; if they expelled demons, so should we; if they planted Spirit-empowered missionary churches, so should we; if they spoke in new tongues, so should we. The book you hold in your hands is written from such an empowerment perspective.

Introduction

For the past two decades, my wife, Sandy, and I have served as Assemblies of God missionaries to Africa. Our ministry has taken us across the continent where we have worked with national church leaders helping them to mobilize their churches for Spirit-empowered missions. In this capacity, we have witnessed with our own eyes what can happen when a local or national church takes seriously the command of Jesus to "stay in the city until you have been clothed with power from on high" (Luke 24:49).

We have observed dormant churches come alive following repeated outpourings of the Spirit. Church planting and missions movements have been launched as churches applied the missional principles found in the Book of Acts to their own context. Two common ingredients found in all of these missions movements are an unwavering commitment to Christ and His mission and an insistence that every member be empowered by the Spirit. Both ideas are found in Jesus final words to His church in Acts 1:8.

The idea for this book was born when I was approached by representatives of the Oral Learners Bible Institute (OLBI) asking me to write a course for them on the Book of Acts. OLBI is an international nonresident ministerial training program for nonreaders. They partner with Christian educators around the world to develop audio Bible school courses for pastors and church leaders who are not able to read. These courses are first produced as scripts. Then, they are recorded and placed on micro SD cards, which can be inserted into cell phones where students can listen to them or watch them in video format. When I was invited to write these scripts, it immediately occurred to me that these lessons could be modified and put into a book form, which I have done.

This book is deigned to take the reader on an exciting 45-day journey through the Book of Acts. Because its original target

Introduction

audience were men and women studying for ministry, the lessons are designed to be very practical.

Each lesson begins by retelling a story from the Book of Acts in contemporary language. It then offers insights into the meaning and background of the text followed by three to five life-lessons the reader can apply to his or her own life and ministry. The book can be used as a daily devotional or as a guide for group study. Because of its strong emphasis on practical application, it can also be used by pastors and teachers as an excellent resource in sermon preparation.

I now commend this book to you. I pray that the Lord of the Harvest will use its lessons to help mold you into the missional servant He has chosen you to be.

Day 1

Introducing Acts

Acts is one of the most exciting books ever written. It tells the story of how the church began. In its pages we learn that the church did not begin timidly, nor apologetically. It began with a mighty explosion of God's power and grace. The Book of Acts is filled with thrilling stories of true commitment and courage. As we move through this study, we will be looking at those stories.

Acts of the Holy Spirit

It has often been said that the title, "The Acts of the Apostles" is not the best name for the book. I agree. A better name might be "The Acts of the Holy Spirit." This is because He is the central character and champion of the entire book. As the story of Acts progresses, the human characters change. For instance, some stories feature Peter; others feature Stephen, and others Paul or someone else. However, the leading character of the book, the Holy Spirit, remains constant. Throughout Acts He takes center stage, filling, empowering, and directing the work.

In Acts, the Holy Spirit is revealed as the Spirit of Missions. Missions is, in fact, a central theme of both Luke's gospel and the

Book of Acts. A question we must each ask ourselves is, "Have I allowed the Holy Spirit to take the center stage in my own life?" We must ensure that we allow Him to have His proper place in our lives and ministries.

Some read Acts only as history. They say, "Wasn't it wonderful how the Spirit worked in the Book of Acts?" However, they do not expect Him to work in the same manner today. Others ask, "Why not today? Why can't the twenty-first century church receive the same Spirit in the same way, and thus experience the same power, glory, and guidance as did the Early Church?" I believe that it can, and should.

Before plunging into the text of Acts, it is important that we take time to ask and answer two important questions. First, "Why should we study Acts?" And second, "Who wrote the Book of Acts?"

Why Study Acts?

We should study Acts for at least three reasons. First, a proper understanding of Acts will help us to understand the rest of the New Testament. Acts serves an important bridge between the Gospels and the New Testament epistles. Just think, if there were no Book of Acts, we would be left wondering who Paul was and where the churches to whom he wrote came from. There would be many gaps in our knowledge of the church, and our understanding of the rest of the New Testament books would be greatly diminished.

Second, we study Acts because it helps us to see what the Early Church looked like, and it gives us a model of what the church should look like today.

Finally, we study Acts because it gives us a divinely inspired strategy for missionary outreach. It is, in fact, a training manual for twenty-first century Christians. Luke intended for the Book of Acts to be a lasting model of how the kingdom of God would advance until Jesus comes again.

Meet the Author

Who wrote the Book of Acts? We know that the Holy Spirit is the author of the entire Bible. Therefore, He is the author of Acts. But which human author did the Holy Spirit inspire to write Acts? The Book of Acts was written by Luke. This is the same Luke who wrote the Gospel of Luke. In Acts we learn that Luke traveled and ministered with Paul during some of his missionary travels. In his letter to the Colossians, Paul called Luke his "dear friend" and identified him as a medical doctor (Col. 4:14).

Although Acts is addressed to a man by the name of Theophilus, it is clear that Luke's message was not just for that one person. It was for a much wider readership. Theophilus was possibly Luke's patron and helped to finance the writing and distribution of the book.

Luke's Purpose in Writing

Why did Luke write the Book of Acts? Certainly, Luke wrote to let his readers know about the beginnings of the church and its eventual spread from Jerusalem to Rome. His primary reason for writing, however, was not simply to teach history. Luke wrote to call the church back to its Pentecostal and missionary roots. By telling these believers the story of how the church began, and how, in the power of the Holy Spirit, it advanced in the face of strong opposition, he hoped to encourage them to do the same. Luke wanted them to know that the same thing could happen to them if they, like those first disciples, would understand the purpose of the church and the necessity of being empowered by the Holy Spirit.

Luke further wrote to teach his readers that the empowering presence of the Spirit comes from a powerful spiritual experience called the baptism in the Holy Spirit (Luke 3:16; Acts 1:5; 11:16). In Acts, Luke shows that this experience is separate from salvation and accompanied by speaking in tongues. Its purpose is to empower believers for effective witness.

The Key to Understanding Acts

Understanding Jesus' words in Acts 1:8 is the key to understanding the entire Book of Acts. We will talk about this more in the next chapter. Right now, it is important that you commit this verse to memory. It reads,

> *"But you will receive power when the Holy Spirit comes on you; and you will be my witnesses in Jerusalem, and in all Judea and Samaria, and to the ends of the earth."*

These are Jesus' final words before He went back to heaven. They help us to understand the Book of Acts in two powerful ways:

First, Jesus' words in Acts 1:8 introduce an important repeated pattern in the book. Jesus said, "You will receive power when the Holy Spirit comes on you; and you will be my witnesses." This pattern, which we call Luke's "empowerment-witness motif," will be repeated again and again throughout Acts. (The word *motif* means pattern.) As we go through these lessons, we will see the Holy Spirit coming upon disciples again and again. And each time He comes upon them, He fills them, and they become powerful witnesses for Christ.

Not only do Jesus' words in Acts 1:8 reveal an empowerment-witness motif in Acts, they also provide an outline—or a sort of table of contents—for the book. Jesus said that His followers would be His witnesses "in Jerusalem, and in all Judea and Samaria, and to the ends of the earth." Using this statement, we can outline the Book of Acts as follows:

- Chapters 1-11 talk about the church's witness in Jerusalem. We call this section the "The Jewish Mission."
- Chapters 8-12 talk about the church's witness in Judea and Samaria. We call this section the "Transitional Period."
- Chapters 13-28 talk about the church's witness to "the ends of the earth." We call this section the "Gentile Mission."

These ideas will become clear as we proceed through this study.

As we conclude this lesson, take a minute to ask the Holy Spirit to come upon you, just as He came upon the disciples in the Book of Acts. Ask Him to fill you, and empower you to be Christ's witness to the lost. When He does, expect to receive power to be Christ's witness to your unsaved family and friends.

Day 1: Introducing Acts

Day 2

Jesus Promises the Spirit

Acts 1:1-14

A wise man once said, "Don't make any promises you don't intend to keep." In today's story Jesus made a promise that He very much intended to keep.

After His resurrection, Jesus spent forty days teaching His disciples about the kingdom of God. One day He met with them and gave them a strong command. He ordered them to stay in Jerusalem until God had given them the gift of the Holy Spirit. "John baptized with water," He said, "but in a few days you will be baptized with the Holy Spirit" (v. 5).

Finally, the day came when He was to leave them and return to heaven. He led them out of the city to the Mount of Olives. There, He told them what would happen to them. He said, "You will receive power when the Holy Spirit comes on you" (v. 8). As a result, they would be given supernatural ability to be powerful witnesses for Him. Their witness would begin in Jerusalem where they were. It would then expand into all of Judea and Samaria, and eventually it would reach the ends of the earth.

Then, something amazing happened. As the disciples watched, Jesus' feet lifted off the ground, and He began to ascend. He went higher and higher until a cloud hid Him from their sight. Awestruck, they stood starring into the sky. Suddenly two angels appeared before them. "Men of Galilee," one angel said, "why do you stand here looking into the sky? This same Jesus, who has been taken from you into heaven, will come back in the same way you have seen Him go into heaven" (v. 11).

The disciples obeyed Jesus' command and went to the upstairs room in Jerusalem where they were staying. There, they all joined together in constant prayer. With them was Mary, the mother of Jesus, His brothers, and some women. In all there were about 120 committed disciples.

From this amazing story we learn five important lessons. These lessons will help us to understand the rest of the Book of Acts. They will also help us in fulfilling the ministries Christ has given us.

Acts is About Missions

The first lesson we learn is concerning the nature of the Book of Acts itself. We learn that Acts is about the church fulfilling God's mission and the necessity of one's being empowered by the Holy Spirit to participate in that mission. Remember Jesus' last command and His last promise to His disciples. His last command was, "Do not leave Jerusalem, but wait for the gift my Father promised… For John baptized with water, but in a few days you will be baptized with the Holy Spirit" (vv. 4-5). His last promise was, "You will receive power when the Holy Spirit has come upon you, and you will be my witnesses in Jerusalem, and in all Judea and Samaria, and to the ends of the earth" (v. 8).

In this promise, Jesus reminded His disciples of their mission; they were to be His witnesses. As we move through Acts, we will discover that the book is primarily about witnessing. Beginning on the Day of Pentecost, and continuing to the end of the book, we will observe the disciples telling people about Jesus. In fact, the words "witness" or "testify" are used more than thirty times in Acts.

Be About Christ's Mission

The second lesson we learn from the opening verses of Acts is about our participation in Jesus' mission to redeem the nations. When Jesus said, "You are to be my witnesses," He was not just talking to His apostles. He was talking to everyone who would choose to follow Him until He returns from heaven. This statement represents the final time Jesus uttered what is known as His "Great Commission."

This commission is recorded five times in Scripture, once in each of the four Gospels and once in Acts:

- In Matthew 28:19-20 Jesus said, "Therefore go and make disciples of all nations, baptizing them in the name of the Father and of the Son and of the Holy Spirit."
- In Mark 16:15, He commanded, "Go into all the world and preach the good news to all creation."
- In Luke 24:47, Jesus told His disciples that "repentance and forgiveness of sins will be preached in his name to all nations."
- In John 20:21, He commissioned them, "As the Father has sent me, I am sending you."
- Now in Acts 1:8 Jesus issues a final command, "You will be my witnesses in Jerusalem, and in all Judea and Samaria, and to the ends of the earth."

Above all else, as disciples of Jesus, we have been called to be His witnesses. We would all do well to memorize these five versions of the Great Commission.

Continue to the Ends of the Earth

The third lesson we learn from the beginning verses of Acts is about the extent of our witness. It is to continue until we reach "the ends of the earth" (v. 8). This statement of Jesus reminds us that God is concerned about every person in every place in the world. We must, therefore, commit ourselves to proclaim the good news about Jesus to all people.

While not every Christian can personally go to the ends of the earth, every follower of Jesus can pray for lost people everywhere. And we can all give our money to help others go. Someone has said that we should "think globally, and act locally." In other words, we should never forget that all over the world people are lost and in need of a Savior. Then, we should do whatever we can to see that they hear the gospel. We can also reach out to people in nearby villages and communities by planting churches there.

Be Empowered by the Holy Spirit

In Acts 1:8, Jesus further tells us how we will be able to carry out our task of reaching our lost world with the gospel. We can do it in the power of the Holy Spirit. Jesus promised, "You will receive power when the Holy Spirit has come upon you, and you will be my witnesses" (v. 8)

As we have said, this pattern of receiving power, then becoming witnesses for Christ, is a pattern that is repeated throughout the Book of Acts. Every time the Spirit comes upon and fills faithful followers of Jesus, they become inspired, effective witnesses—and the kingdom

Day 2: Jesus Promises the Spirit

of God advances. As we move through this study of the Book of Acts, we will discover seven "key outpourings" of the Holy Spirit that dramatically make this point.

Those seven outpourings of the Spirit take place

- in Jerusalem (2:1-4),
- in Jerusalem again (4:31),
- in Samaria (8:15-17),
- in Damascus (9:17-18),
- in Caesarea (10:44-47),
- in Antioch (13:1-4),
- and in Ephesus (19:6).

You may want to pause and read these passages in the Book of Acts for yourself. Each outpouring emphasizes the "empowerment-witness motif" we discussed in the last lesson.

During the forty days between His resurrection and His ascension, Jesus repeatedly told His disciples to "Go!" But now He tells them to "Stay!" In other words, they must "go into all the worlds and preach the good news to all creation" (Mark 16:15), but first, they must "stay" in Jerusalem and "wait for the gift [His] Father promised" (Acts 1:4).

What important lesson do we learn from this story? We learn that before one can effectively obey His first command (to go and preach the gospel), he or she will need to obey His second command (to be baptized in the Holy Spirit). Jesus has left us with a humanly impossible task—the evangelization of all nations before He comes again. It is a job beyond our ability. Therefore, we must have supernatural help. We, like those first disciples of Jesus, must wait in the city until we have been "clothed with power from on high" (Luke 24:49).

Day 2: Jesus Promises the Spirit

Continue Until Jesus Comes

The last lesson concerns how long our witness is to continue. As the disciples looked on, Jesus was taken up into heaven. The angels appeared and challenged them, "Men of Galilee, why do you stand here looking into the sky? This same Jesus…will come back in the same way you have seen him go into heaven" (v. 11). Remember, Jesus had just commanded the disciples to return to Jerusalem and wait to receive power from on high. They were to quickly obey. They had no time to waste staring into heaven. Since Jesus will come back, there is an urgency about our mission to reach the lost. We must go quickly to the harvest fields (Luke 14:21).

As we conclude today's lesson, take a moment and pray. Commit yourself to God and His mission. Then ask God to give you His Spirit to empower you for the task.

Day 3

Pentecost: The Spirit is Poured Out

Acts 2:1-13

Have you ever stood under a waterfall and let the water pour down upon you from above? Could this have been how the disciples felt on the Day of Pentecost when Jesus poured the Holy Spirit on them?

In obedience to Jesus' command, 120 of His faithful followers, including the apostles, gathered in Jerusalem to wait for the gift of the Holy Spirit. For just over a week these men and women continued in prayer and praise to God. Great expectation filled their hearts. When the Day of Pentecost arrived, they gathered in the temple for prayer. Possibly they met under one of the covered porticoes to one side of the huge Court of the Gentiles. There they sat down, and as the festive crowds milled around them, they began their prayers.

That's when it all happened! Suddenly from heaven came a thunderous roar—like the sound of a powerful windstorm. In wonder, the people's eyes turned skyward. Some clasped their hands over their ears to mute the deafening sound. Then, as suddenly as it had begun,

Day 3: Pentecost: The Spirit is Poured Out

the noise stopped. Everyone stood in quiet astonishment, wondering what had just happened.

Then, without warning a huge mass of flames appeared above the heads of the 120. Soon, the mass of flames began to divide itself into smaller "tongues" of fire. One fiery tongue settled on the head of each disciple. The onlookers watched in amazement. In the meantime, those in the vicinity who had heard the heavenly sound began rushing into the temple court where the disciples were praying. The crowd quickly grew into the thousands.

As everyone stood marveling at the wind and the fire, God worked yet another wonder. The Bible says that "all of [the 120 disciples] were filled with the Holy Spirit and began to speak in other tongues as the Spirit enabled them" (v. 4). Incredibly, they were speaking in languages they had not learned.

To some in the crowd it seemed as if these poor Galileans were drunk. "They are full of sweet wine!" someone shouted. However, as the people listened more closely, one by one, they began to hear these uneducated Galileans speaking in their own native languages. Visitors from Arabia heard them speaking Arabic; those from Egypt heard them speaking Coptic; others from Rome heard them speaking Latin, and so it went. What were they saying? They were boldly proclaiming the mighty deeds of God! Dumbfounded, the people asked, "What does this mean?"

The Festival of Pentecost

For the Jews of Jesus' day, the Festival of Pentecost was one of three important annual feasts in which every Jewish male in the area was required to attend. The word "Pentecost" means fiftieth. Thus, Pentecost took place fifty days after Passover. In the Old Testament, the festival is called by three different names: the Feast of Weeks

Day 3: Pentecost: The Spirit is Poured Out

(Exodus 34:22), the Feast of Harvest (23:16), and the Feast of Firstfruits (23:19). Thousands of Jewish pilgrims gathered from all over the Roman Empire to attend this annual feast.

For Christians, Pentecost has a different meaning. It is one of the most significant events in all of history. It was on that day that God first empowered His church to carry the message of Christ the ends of the earth. Without this powerful infilling, the early disciples would never have been able to accomplish the mission God had given them. The same is true today. Without the empowering of the Holy Spirit it will be impossible for us to take the gospel to all nations before Jesus comes again.

The outpouring of the Spirit at Pentecost is also the defining event of the Book of Acts. It sets the stage for everything that follows. A clear understanding of the meaning and purpose of Pentecost is essential for a correct understanding of the rest of the Book of Acts.

The Wonders of Pentecost

The outpouring of the Spirit at Pentecost was accompanied by two great supernatural wonders. The first wonder was a sound from heaven "like the blowing of a violent wind" (v. 2). It was a sign from God that He had come powerfully on the scene. Weeks earlier, on the night of His resurrection, Jesus had breathed on His eleven disciples and told them to "receive the Holy Spirit" (John 20:21). Now, God is breathing on the 120 at Pentecost, and His breath sounds like a mighty wind from heaven!

This sound of wind from heaven also speaks to the missionary purpose of the Spirit's outpouring. Wind is a powerful force of nature. Jesus said that the global missionary work of the church is to be carried out in the power of the Spirit. In John 3:8, He described the Spirit's work as being like the wind. The Spirit works tirelessly throughout the world inspiring and empowering the church, revealing Christ to the lost and drawing people unto Him.

A second wonder occurred at Pentecost. What looked like tongues of fire appeared and came to rest on each of the 120 disciples. It was a sign that the Holy Spirit was coming upon the disciples to empower them as witnesses. By empowering them with the Spirit, He would set their tongues aflame to proclaim the gospel to the lost.

The Power of Pentecost

The Holy Spirit, who had come powerfully into the world, and amazingly upon the disciples, now enters into them and fills them with His power and presence. The Bibles says, "All of them were filled with the Holy Spirit and began to speak in other tongues as the Spirit enabled them" (Acts 2:4).

The purpose of their being filled with the Spirit was not to for their conversion, but to empower them to witness—just as Jesus had promised in Acts 1:8. Notice further that they were all filled with the Spirit. It is noteworthy that, in Acts, every time the Spirit of God is poured out on a group of people, they are all filled. This shows us that the baptism in the Holy Spirit is an experience for all believers. Every believer must be empowered by the Spirit because every believer is called to be Christ's witness (Acts 1:8).

The Tongues of Pentecost

The immediate effect of the disciples' being filled with the Holy Spirit at Pentecost was that they "began to speak in tongues as the Spirit enabled them" (v. 4). This is the first of three times in the Book of Acts that people are said to speak in tongues. (The other two times are at Cornelius' home in Caesarea in Acts 10:46 and in Ephesus in

Day 3: Pentecost: The Spirit is Poured Out

Acts 19:6.) Each time, their speaking in tongues happened immediately after they were filled with the Spirit.

In is important to notice that the first two signs of Pentecost (the sound from heaven and the tongues of fire) preceded the disciples' being filled with the Spirit, and they are never repeated in the Book of Acts. The third sign (speaking in tongues) immediately followed their being filled with the Spirit, and it is repeated two more times in the Book of Acts.

In Acts, Luke presents speaking in tongues is the "initial physical evidence" or the "normative missional sign" (my preferred phrase) that one has been baptized in the Holy Spirit. In other words, when someone speaks in tongues, it is a sign from God that they have been empowered to be Christ's witness to the lost.

The fact that the disciples at Pentecost spoke in fifteen Gentile languages also testifies to the missionary purpose of the gift of the Holy Spirit. The purpose of the baptism in the Holy Spirit is empower Christ's disciples to be His witnesses "in Jerusalem, and in all Judea and Samaria, and to the ends of the earth" (Acts 1:8).

Have you been baptized in the Holy Spirit with the missional sign of speaking in tongues as the Spirit enables? If you haven't, then ask God to fill you with His Spirit today. If you have, then go out and tell someone about Jesus expecting the Holy Spirit to empower your witness.

Day 3: Pentecost: The Spirit is Poured Out

Day 4

Pentecost: Peter's Spirit-Inspired Message

Acts 2:14-41

The crowd who had gathered in the temple court for the Pentecost celebrations couldn't believe their eyes—or their ears! When they saw the miracles of Pentecost, including the 120 disciples' speaking in tongues, they cried out, "What does this mean?"

Peter was now full of the Holy Spirit, so he rose to answer their question. "These men are not drunk, as you are saying," he declared. "After all, it's only nine in the morning." In fact, just the opposite was true; they had all been filled with the Spirit!

Peter then told the people how this miracle had been foretold by Joel. Centuries before, the prophet had written, "In the last days, God says, I will pour out my Spirit on all people. Your sons and daughters will prophesy" (v 17). Peter explained how these disciples' filling with the Spirit, and their speaking in tongues, was a fulfillment of this ancient prophecy.

Peter further explained to the crowd that this powerful experience from God was not just for these disciples; it was for all of God's people—until Jesus comes again. It was for men and women, young and old, rich and poor. And because God was freely pouring out His Spirit on all people, the door of salvation had been opened. Now, "everyone who calls on the name of the Lord will be saved" (v. 21).

Once Peter had explained to the people what had happened, he began to boldly proclaim the gospel to them. He told them about Jesus' miracles, His crucifixion, His resurrection, and His exaltation to the right hand of God. He then explained how all of these things were part of God's plan from the beginning. What they had just witnessed was proof of this. Jesus, whom they had crucified, had ascended to the right hand of God. There He had received from the Father the promise of the Spirit, and now He had poured out the Holy Spirit on these disciples. Peter concluded his message, ""Therefore let all Israel be assured of this: God has made this Jesus, whom you crucified, both Lord and Christ" (v. 36).

When the people heard Peter's Spirit-inspired words, they were deeply moved. They began to cry out to the apostles, "Brothers, what shall we do?" Peter replied, "The promise [of the Holy Spirit] is for you and your children and for all who are far off—for all whom the Lord our God will call" (v. 39). They must first repent of their sins and follow Christ in water baptism.

Because of the powerful demonstrations at Pentecost, and Peter's powerful proclamation of the gospel, about three thousand people repented of their sins and put their faith in Christ. They were baptized in water and added to the church that very day.

Prophecy is Fulfilled

At Pentecost the people asked, "What does this mean?" Peter responded by explaining that the Spirit's outpouring at Pentecost was not to be thought of as a random event. It was, rather, a fulfillment of

Day 4: Pentecost: Peter's Spirit-Inspired Message

an ancient prophecy. It was part of God's eternal plan to redeem the nations. Joel had prophesied that God would one day pour out His Spirit on all people. When that day came, the door would be opened for all people to be saved. God was fulfilling these ancient prophecies before their eyes.

Another prophecy was being fulfilled at Pentecost. This is the prediction Jesus had made about a week before. He had told His disciples that they would receive power when the Holy Spirit came upon them. As a result, they would become powerful witnesses for Christ. At Pentecost this promise was first fulfilled. Peter, along with the rest of the 120, was filled with the Spirit. Immediately, he began to witness by the Spirit's power. Peter was not merely speaking out of his own heart; he was speaking by the Spirit and telling the people about Jesus.

The Gospel Proclaimed

Peter's Spirit-anointed message at Pentecost (along with his message in Acts 3) establishes a pattern for preaching the gospel in Acts. We should follow this pattern today. Peter's message includes the following key elements.

- First, Peter announced that Jesus was Lord and that He was crucified, raised from the dead, and exalted to the right hand of God (2:22-36; 3:13-15).
- Second, he announced that the Spirit has been poured out on all believers (2:16-18, 32-33; 3:19).
- Third, Peter encouraged the people to receive the promised gift of the Holy Spirit (2:38-39).
- Fourth, he declared that Jesus will return (3:20-21).
- Finally, he called on the people to repent of their sins and put their faith in Christ for salvation (2:36-38; 3:19).

Day 4: Pentecost: Peter's Spirit-Inspired Message

Each of these five elements should be found in our preaching today. Christ's death, burial, and resurrection must be at the heart of all our preaching (see 1 Cor. 15:1-7). We must never forget that it is this message, preached in the power of the Spirit, which will open the door for people to be saved. We must also proclaim that Jesus baptizes in the Holy Spirit and empowers His disciples to witness for Him. And we must announce that Jesus is coming again. We would be very foolish and shortsighted if we were to replace this message with other less important messages, no matter how appealing they may seem at the time.

The Spirit Promised

Those who listened to Peter's Spirit-anointed message were "cut to the heart," that is, they were brought under strong conviction by the Holy Spirit (see John 16:8-11). Such conviction is the natural result of the gospel being proclaimed in the power of the Holy Spirit.

The people then asked the apostles, "What shall we do?" They were asking, "What must we do to receive Christ and to experience what we have seen here today?" Peter answered them, "Repent and be baptized, every one of you, in the name of Jesus Christ for the forgiveness of your sins. And you will receive the gift of the Holy Spirit" (Acts 2:38).

We should not confuse the "gift of the Holy Spirit" that Peter is talking about here with the "gifts of the Holy Spirit" that Paul talks about in his letters. This "gift of the Spirit" is the gift of the Spirit himself. It is an empowering experience from God, separate from conversion, given to Jesus' disciples to empower them to witness for Him.

Peter then told the people that this promise of the Spirit "is for you and your children and for all who are far off—for all whom the

Lord our God will call" (v. 39). In other words, the gift of the Spirit is for all people of every generation until Jesus comes again.

Three Thousand Saved

As a result of the outpouring of the Spirit at Pentecost and Peter's Spirit-empowered witness that followed, three thousand people were saved and added to the church. This showed that Jesus' promise was true. He had promised the church power to fulfil its mission of proclaiming Christ "in Jerusalem, and in all Judea, and Samaria, and to the ends of the earth" (1:8).

Now that promise was being fulfilled. As a result of the Spirit coming upon and filling Peter and the other disciples at Pentecost, the church began witnessing with great power. In one day, three thousand people committed their lives to Jesus Christ and were added to the church.

As disciples of Jesus, we must be ever mindful of our two great kingdom responsibilities. First, we must clearly proclaim the gospel of Christ and point people to salvation. Second, we must immediately lead these same people into the baptism in the Holy Spirit. Being born of the Spirit will prepare them for heaven. Being filled with the Spirit will prepare them for Christian service.

Day 4: Pentecost: Peter's Spirit-Inspired Message

Day 5

More Lessons from Pentecost

In Africa a young man was studying the Book of Acts. As he studied, he discovered how the apostles preached with power, and how God confirmed their preaching with miracles, signs, and wonders. He also learned about how they planted Spirit-empowered missionary churches and advanced God's kingdom into new regions. He became very excited and said to himself, "I want to be like the apostles and early Christians." He then told Jesus, "If you will help me, I will someday do the things they did."

One day he went to his pastor and told him about his desire to be used by God. The pastor reminded him of what he was learning from the Book of Acts. If he wanted to do the same works as the apostles, he would need to be empowered by the Spirit as the apostles. The pastor then prayed with the young man, and he was wondrously baptized in the Holy Spirit and he began to speak in tongues, just like the 120 disciples did on the Day of Pentecost.

The young man's life began to change. His compassion for the lost grew. As time passed, the Lord gave him a burden for a nearby village. Again, he went to his pastor. This time he asked if he could take a team from the church and go the village and plant a new church there. The pastor agreed.

The young man and his team went to the village and conducted a church planting campaign. The Lord anointed his preaching and performed miracles to confirm the message. People were saved, and today there is a strong church in that place. In time, teams went out from the new church and started even more churches in the area. This is a wonderful example of how we can put into action the lessons we are studying in this book.

Before we conclude our study of the Day of Pentecost, we will discuss three important issues. First, we will address how the outpouring of the Spirit at Pentecost fulfills Jesus' promise in Acts 1:8. Next, we examine the missionary focus of the Day of Pentecost. Finally, we will learn how we can receive the Holy Spirit into our own lives today.

Pentecost: The First Jerusalem Outpouring

In Acts 1:8 Jesus promised His disciples, "You will receive power when the Holy Spirit comes on you; and you will be my witnesses in Jerusalem…" Remember, the outpouring of the Spirit at Pentecost occurred in Jerusalem. And as Jesus had promised, the result was powerful Spirit-empowered witness in the city. Thus, what happened on the Day of Pentecost is the first great example in Acts of the empowerment-witness motif Jesus described in Acts 1:8: "You will receive power…and you will be my witnesses."

It is possible to see the outpouring of the Spirit at Pentecost in two distinct ways—both of which are true. First, the outpouring of the Spirit at Pentecost can be viewed as a onetime historical event. Just as there was only one Calvary and one resurrection of Jesus, historically speaking, there was only one Day of Pentecost.

However, what happened at Pentecost was more than a historical event. It can also be viewed as a typical outpouring of the Spirit on a local congregation of believers. As such, it can be expected to occur again and again throughout the Book of Acts—and throughout church history.

At Pentecost the church in Jerusalem was empowered by the Spirit to carry out its task of witnessing for Christ "in Jerusalem." It is an example of how any church needs to go about reaching its city or village with the gospel. Like those first disciples, they must first commit themselves to God's mission and then be empowered by the Holy Spirit.

The outpouring of the Spirit on the church in Jerusalem is also the first example of the empowerment-witness motif (pattern) in Acts, as mentioned earlier. As we go through Acts, we will point out how this pattern is repeated again and again.

Also, as we discussed on Day 1, the outpouring of the Spirit at Pentecost launched the "Jewish Mission." The Jewish Mission involves reaching Jerusalem with the gospel. It continues through Acts 7. Further, as discussed on Day 2, Pentecost is the first of seven key outpourings of the Spirit in Acts.

Pentecost is about Missions

It is important that we understand that the Day of Pentecost was a truly missionary event. Everything that happened on that day emphasizes this truth. Observe these six amazing facts about the Day of Pentecost:

- *Fact 1: The Promise of Pentecost.* Jesus' promise concerning Pentecost was a missionary promise. Remember, before the Day of Pentecost He told His disciples, "But you will receive power when the Holy Spirit comes on you; and you will be my witnesses in Jerusalem, and in all Judea and Samaria, and to the ends of the earth" (1:8).

Day 5: More Lessons from Pentecost

- *Fact 2: The Timing of Pentecost.* The outpouring of the Spirit at Pentecost occurred on a harvest festival known to the Jews as the Feast of Harvest (Exod. 23:22). Pentecost thus represented the beginning of God's worldwide harvest of souls. In His parables, Jesus often spoke of harvest and missions.
- *Fact 3: The Sign of Pentecost.* When the 120 Jewish disciples were filled with the Spirit on the Day of Pentecost, they began "declaring the wonders of God" in Gentile languages (2:11). By choosing this sign, God was showing His church that He wanted all nations to hear the gospel.
- *Fact 4: The Setting of Pentecost.* The Bible says that on the Day of Pentecost there were in Jerusalem "God-fearing Jews from every nation under heaven" (2:5). This fact helps us to understand that Pentecost was an international gathering with an international purpose.
- *Fact 5: Peter's Explanation of Pentecost.* Peter explained to the crowd at Pentecost that they were witnessing a fulfillment of Joel's prophecy that God would pour out His Spirit "on all people" (2:17). In using the term "all people," the prophet was talking about people from every nation and place in the world.
- *Fact 6: The Results of Pentecost.* As a result of the outpouring of the Spirit at Pentecost, and Peter's Spirit-empowered witness, 3,000 people were saved from "every nation under heaven" (2:41).

So you see, everything that happened on the Day of Pentecost was about God empowering and preparing His church to take the gospel to the ends of the earth. The same is true today. We seek for a Pentecostal outpouring in our churches, not so we can become more blessed, but so that we can be empowered and prepared to participate in God's last-days harvest.

Day 5: More Lessons from Pentecost

How to Be Filled with the Spirit

An important question we must answer at this point in our study is "How can we today receive the same empowering experience the disciples received on the Day of Pentecost 2,000 years ago?" Jesus answers this question in Luke 11:9-13. One receives the Spirit by simply asking in faith.

It is helpful to break the process of receiving the Spirit into three simple "faith steps" as follows:

- *Step 1: Ask in faith.* To receive the Spirit, simply and sincerely present your request to God. Jesus promised, "Ask and it will be given you" (Luke 11:9). As you ask, believe that God is hearing and answering your prayer. Confidently pray, "Lord, I believe your promise. I believe that if I ask You for the Spirit, You will give me the Spirit. So, right now, in Jesus' name, I ask You, give me the Holy Spirit, and empower me as Your witness." As you pray, believe that God is giving you His Spirit. Sense the Spirit's presence as He comes upon you.
- *Step 2: Receive by faith.* Once the Spirit comes upon you, you must receive Him inside you. You do this by fully believing Jesus' promise: "Everyone who asks receives" (Luke 11:10). Jesus told us how this is done when He said, "Whatever you ask for in prayer, believe that you have received it, and it will be yours" (Mark 11:24). This act of faith can be compared to Peter's step of faith when he stepped from the boat and began to walk on water (Matt. 14:25-29). His bold step of faith resulted in a miracle! Once you have sensed the Spirit's presence within, in faith make this simple confession: "I am now full of the Holy Spirit!" Consciously sense the Spirit's presence inside you.
- *Step 3: Speak in Faith.* Now, speak as the Spirit enables (see Acts 2:4). Allow the Holy Spirit to gush forth from deep inside, out of

your "innermost being" (John 7:38, NASB). As He does, cooperate with what He is doing. Yield your vocal organs and lips to the Spirit of God. You will begin to speak words in a language you have never learned. When this happens, don't be afraid. This is God's sign to you that He is empowering you to be His witness. Now, yield yourself more and more to the Spirit. Let the words flow. Continue to speak, believing God with all of your heart, holding nothing back, fully trusting God to do His part.

Praise the Lord! You have been baptized in the Holy Spirit, and you have been empowered as Christ's Spirit-anointed spokesperson just as Peter was on the Day of Pentecost. Now, go out and tell someone about Jesus.

Day 6

A New Prophetic Community

Acts 2:41-47

Have you ever met someone whose life was dramatically changed through a powerful encounter with God? This is what happened to people in the Book of Acts. They encountered Christ, and their lives were forever changed.

You will remember from our last lesson how, on the Day of Pentecost, Peter preached with great power. As a result, 3,000 people repented and were added to the church. These new followers of Jesus were soon filled with the Spirit just like Peter and the original 120. As a result of these experiences with God, something wonderful happened. Their lives were changed, and a new prophetic community was born. It was a community of people who were filled with—and whose lives were directed by—the Holy Spirit.

This new community reflected the character and mission of Jesus. For example, they stopped thinking about their own needs. Instead, they devoted themselves to God and to one another. They would often come together to pray and to encourage one another. In their gatherings they encountered the power of the Holy Spirit, and they listened to the apostles teach from the Word of God. God also worked signs and wonders among them. Because of these things, these new believers lived with a sense of holy awe.

Their new prophetic community was one of peace and harmony. Everyone shared what they had, and if anyone had a need, others helped them out. They made it their habit to gather in the temple courts daily for a time of worship and prayer. And they opened their homes to share meals with one another. As a result, their lives were filled with joy and praise.

The people of Jerusalem took notice of how these followers of Jesus acted, and they were attracted to them. They wanted to be a part of this amazing community of believers. Because of these things, people were being saved every day and the church continued to grow.

A Prophetic Community

Jesus did not come to earth simply to teach people how to live better lives. He did do that—but He came for an even greater purpose. He came to establish His kingdom in the earth and in the lives of His followers. It would be a kingdom in which He reigned and His Spirit dwelt.

In the days following the outpouring of the Spirit at Pentecost, the church emerged as a new kind of community—one like the world had never seen before. It was a community of Spirit-anointed prophets. Centuries before Moses had declared, "I wish that all the Lord's people were prophets and that the Lord would put his Spirit on them!" (Num. 11:29).

This is exactly what occurred at Pentecost. Peter used an ancient prophecy spoken by Joel to explain to the crowd what had happened. Joel had said, "In the last days, God says, I will pour out my Spirit on all people. Your sons and daughters will prophesy" (v. 17; Joel 2:28). In other words, at Pentecost God was creating a new community of

Spirit-anointed prophets. What an amazing thing! God's new prophetic people would live and speak by the Spirit.

As we move through the Book of Acts, we will see these followers of Jesus speaking words given to them by the Holy Spirit. Sometimes they will speak in tongues; at other times, they will speak in the common language. However, the main form of prophetic speech occurring in Acts is Spirit-empowered proclamation of the gospel.

However, these new prophetic people will do more than speak by the Spirit; they will live by the Spirit. In other words, they will live as Jesus had lived when He was with them. This new community is a good example of how God wants our churches to be today.

Our story reveals at least four characteristics of this new prophetic community:

A Transformed Community

First, our story reveals that this new prophetic community was a *transformed community.* The people in this new community had encountered the living Christ. As a result, their lives had been dramatically transformed. In Peter's Pentecost sermon, he had told them about Jesus' death and resurrection. He then called on them to repent and believe on Christ. They obeyed and were baptized in water. Their baptism indicates that they had died to their old lives and risen to new life in Christ, and that they had fully committed themselves to Christ and His mission.

A Spirit-empowered Community

Second, our story reveals that this new prophetic community was a *Spirit-empowered community.* These people had not only been transformed by a personal encounter with Christ, they had been empowered through dynamic encounter with the Holy Spirit. In his sermon, Peter had urged them, "Repent and be baptized, every one of you, in the name of Jesus Christ for the forgiveness of your sins, and you will receive the gift of the Holy Spirit" (v. 38). They received Peter's message, repented, and were baptized in water. They then received the gift of the Holy Spirit as Peter had promised.

Because of their experience with the Holy Spirit, these early Christians were equipped to fulfil the mission that Christ had given them. When they gathered for prayer and worship, the Spirit often manifested His presence in their midst. And "everyone kept feeling a sense of awe; and many wonders and signs were taking place through the apostles" (v. 43).

A Devoted Community

Third, our story reveals that this new prophetic community was a *devoted community.* They were devoted to Christ, and were fully prepared to commit themselves and their possessions to those things they knew were most important to Him. They were further devoted to the apostles' teaching, to prayer, and to one another. This shared devotion resulted in great generosity, unity, and gladness of heart.

A Witnessing Community

Finally, our story reveals that this new prophetic community was a *witnessing community.* Jesus had promised, "You will receive power when the Holy Spirit comes on you; and you will be my witnesses" (Acts 1:8). Each passing day these early disciples came to better understand what Jesus had meant. They realized that they would need to carry out their ministries just as Jesus had carried out His, in the power of the Holy Spirit.

So, following Jesus' example, they witnessed in three ways: with their words, with their lives, and through mighty signs and wonders. Because of this three-fold witness, "the Lord added to their number daily those who were being saved" (v. 47).

Our churches today should strive to be like the prophetic community that emerged after the outpouring of the Spirit at Pentecost. While we surely witness with our words, we should never forget that our witness involves more than just words. It also involves being the community of Christ.

As God's prophetic people, our association with one another and the world must be marked by devotion to Christ, to one another, and to the word of God. Our gatherings should be filled with the presence of God and the joy of the Lord. Christ must be at the center of all we do, and His presence should be manifested by wonders and miraculous signs. Such a church will be a powerful witness to those outside and will draw people to itself.

Day 6: A New Prophetic Community

Day 7

Miracle at the Beautiful Gate

Acts 3:1-4:4

Have you ever seen God perform a miracle? If so, how did you feel? How did the people with you respond? In this lesson, we will look at a wonderful miracle that took place soon after the Day of Pentecost. We will also look at the reactions of the people who witnessed the miracle. In doing this, we will learn some important lessons for our own lives and ministries.

One morning Peter and John were on their way to the temple to pray. They had to pass through a huge gate in the inner wall of the temple known as the Beautiful Gate. As they were about to enter, they met a crippled man who asked them for money.

Peter had been filled with the Spirit a few days earlier. Now, as he looked at the crippled man, he sensed that God wanted to heal him. He said to the man, "Look at us!" The man looked at the apostles expectantly. Peter then told him, "I do not have any money, but what I do have I give to you. In the name of Jesus Christ of Nazareth, walk!"

Reaching down, Peter took the man by the right hand, and lifted him up. Instantly the man was healed. Feeling strength come into his ankles and feet, he jumped up and began running through the temple courts, praising God with a loud voice. When the people recognized who this was, they were astounded. They gathered around the apostles and the beggar who was clinging to Peter.

As he had done on the Day of Pentecost, Peter seized the opportunity and began to preach to the crowd. "Why do you wonder at this," he asked, "and why do you stare at us, as though by our own power or godliness we have made this man walk? We did not do this miracle; Jesus did it. He is the very One you rejected and crucified." Peter continued, "You may have killed Him, but God raised Him from the dead!"

Peter then declared the gospel to them, saying that Jesus' death and resurrection had been foretold by the prophets. He called on them to turn to from their sins. If they would do this, God would forgive them and send "times of refreshing" upon them. Peter further urged the people to look for Jesus to come again from heaven. All of this, he said, had been predicted by the holy prophets. God had even promised Abraham that through his offspring—that is, through Jesus—all the peoples of the earth would be blessed. However, they must now repent or be cut off from God's blessings.

When the ruling authorities heard what Peter was saying, they became angry. They didn't want the people to hear about Jesus and His resurrection. So they seized Peter and John and put them in jail. Nevertheless, many of those who heard Peter's message believed, and the number of the men in the church grew to about five thousand.

We can learn two important lessons from this story. First, we learn some things about how we are to witness for Christ. Then, we can learn about how we can expect people to respond to our witness.

How We are to Witness

From today's story we learn five important lessons about how we are to witness for Christ:

1. Seize every opportunity. First, we learn that we must seize every opportunity to witness. That's what Peter did at the Beautiful Gate. As he had done on the Day of Pentecost, when he saw the people beginning to gather, he moved into action. Peter knew that God was again opening a door for him to tell people about Jesus. And because they had witnessed another mighty work of God, they were ready to listen. We, too, should be prepared to witness for Christ whenever God opens the door.

2. Witness in the Spirit's power. Second, we learn that we must witness by the power of the Holy Spirit. On the Day of Pentecost, Peter had been filled with the Holy Spirit. Now, at the Beautiful Gate, he told the lame man, "What I have I give to you." He was talking about the power of the Spirit he had received at Pentecost.

3. Minister in Jesus' name. Third, we learn that we must witness in the name of Jesus. When Peter healed the crippled man, he said to him, "In the name of Jesus Christ of Nazareth rise up and walk." Peter understood the power of Jesus' name (Mark 16:17). To minister in the name of Jesus means to minister under His authority, and to do the things He has commanded us to do. As Peter and the other disciples submitted themselves to Jesus and His mission, they received authority from Him to act in His name.

Today, we must do the same thing. We must be able to say to nonbelievers in need, "What I have I give to you." In other words, we must remain full of the Holy Spirit and submitted to Jesus. Then, when opportunities present themselves, we will be able to minister to them.

4. Proclaim the gospel. Fourth, from our story we learn that we must faithfully proclaim the gospel of Christ. As he had done at Pentecost, Peter again told the people about Jesus. He told them how Jesus died on the cross and how God raised Him from the dead. He then called on them to trust in Christ and repent of their sins.

As we go about, it is not enough that we simply "preach the Bible." Certainly, we must do that; however, we must remember to keep our message centered on Christ. We must clearly explain the meaning of His death and resurrection. And we must call the people to faith and repentance.

5. Expect miracles. Finally, from our story we learn that, when we witness for Christ, we can expect God to miraculously confirm His word. God healed the crippled man to prove that Jesus was alive and that His kingdom had come in power. The healing also confirmed that the gospel message was true.

God will do the same for us today. If we will be filled with the Holy Spirit, submit ourselves to Christ's authority, and boldly proclaim the gospel, we can expect the Lord to empower our message and to confirm His word by performing miraculous signs.

How People Respond

Not only does the story of the healing of the man at the Beautiful Gate teach us how we should witness for Christ, it also teaches us a couple of things about how we can expect people to respond to our witness.

1. Some will oppose. First, our story teaches us that we can expect some to oppose the gospel. On the Day of Pentecost, some of the people mocked the disciples. Now, at the Beautiful Gate the Jewish authorities opposed the apostles as they preached the gospel.

It is the same today. Not everyone we witness to will welcome our message. Some may even oppose us. Whatever the case, we must faithfully share the message of Christ with all.

2. Some will believe. However, our story teaches us a second and even more important lesson. It teaches us that, while some will oppose the message, others will believe and put their faith in Jesus. The Jewish rulers opposed the message, but many of the common people received it with joy. In a short time, the number of men in the church in Jerusalem grew to 5,000. If you add women and children to that number, the number of people in the church could have been as many as 20,000—or even more. When He was with them, Jesus had promised His disciples, "Do not be afraid. From now on you will catch men" (Luke 5:10, NKJV).

The same is true today. If we will faithfully proclaim the message of the gospel, the Holy Spirit will work, and some will receive the message and put their faith in Christ.

Day 7: Miracle at the Beautiful Gate

Day 8

Bold Witness Before the Jewish Leaders

Acts 4:5-22

In many places in the world, believers are being persecuted for their faith in Christ. How about you? Have you ever been persecuted for preaching the gospel? How did it make you feel? How did you respond to the persecution? In the Book of Acts, disciples were often persecuted for preaching the gospel. Our story today is the first instance of such persecution, but as we will discover, it was not the last.

Following the outpouring of the Spirit at Pentecost, the disciples in Jerusalem became powerful witnesses for Christ. Everywhere they went, they told people about Jesus. God confirmed their message by working miracles through them. On one occasion, Peter and John healed a cripple man right inside the temple courtyard.

Because of their Spirit-empowered witness, the church grew quickly. Each day more people became followers of Jesus. And each day the Jewish leaders became more agitated. This new movement was threatening their authority, and they wanted it stopped. So they seized Peter and John and put them in jail.

Day 8: Bold Witness Before the Jewish Leaders

The next day the high priest called a meeting of the Jewish high council known as the Sanhedrin. He then had Peter and John brought in for questioning. He asked the two apostles, "Who gave you the authority to preach about Jesus and stir up the people?"

Peter was again filled with the Spirit, just he had been on the Day of Pentecost. And again he spoke with power and courage. "Why are you examining us?" he asked. Then, pointing at the man who had been healed, he asked, "Is it because we have healed this crippled man? Isn't that a good thing?"

Peter then declared, "It is by the name of Jesus Christ of Nazareth, whom you crucified but whom God raised from the dead, that this man stands before you healed" (Acts 4:10). Jesus is the stone the builders rejected, but now God has made Him the capstone. Then, Peter said something very important about Jesus. "Salvation is found in no one else," he declared, "for there is no other name under heaven given to men by which we must be saved" (v. 12).

The Jewish leaders who were listening to Peter were astonished. How could these ordinary men speak with such power and eloquence? Then they realized, it was because they had been with Jesus. However, since the man who had been healed was standing there with them, they could say nothing.

After Peter had finished speaking, the Jewish leaders gathered for a meeting. They wondered aloud, "What are we going to do with these men? Everybody living in Jerusalem knows they have done an outstanding miracle, and we cannot deny it" (v. 16). They decided to threaten them and let them go. So they called them in and warned them not to speak any more in Jesus' name.

However, Peter and John were full of the Spirit, so they answered boldly, "Judge for yourselves whether it is right in God's sight to obey you rather than God. For we cannot help speaking about what we have seen and heard" (vv. 19-20). Not knowing how to answer them, the Jewish leaders threatened them some more, and sent them away.

Sometimes we too are persecuted for witnessing for Christ. At such times, we must remain faithful to Him and to the mission He has given us. From this story, we learn three important lessons about how we are to respond when we are opposed or threatened for preaching the gospel:

Stay Full of the Spirit

The first lesson we learn is that, as Christ's disciples, we must be filled with—and remain full of—the Holy Spirit. When Peter was captured and questioned for telling people about Jesus, he was filled with the Holy Spirit (4:8). You will remember that this was not the first time Peter was filled with the Spirit. He was first filled on the Day of Pentecost. Now, he is refilled with the Spirit. In other words, the Holy Spirit comes and anoints him, giving him boldness to speak and wisdom to know what to say.

When Jesus was still with His disciples, He had told them, "When you are brought before...rulers and authorities, do not worry about how you will defend yourselves or what you will say, for the Holy Spirit will teach you at that time what you should say" (Luke 12:11-12). Now, the Spirit was keeping that promise. And because the two apostles were full of the Spirit, they could not stop speaking about Jesus.

It is the same with us today. If we will remain full of the Holy Spirit, He will empower us and sustain us during times of persecution. We can make sure we remain full of the Spirit through prayer, openness to God, and repeated infillings of the Holy Spirit.

Obey God

A second lesson we learn from this story is that we must always obey God rather than men. When ordered to stop preaching in Jesus' name, Peter and John answered, "We must obey God rather than men" (v. 29). Certainly, we must obey the laws of society. The Bible clearly teaches that. However, as citizens of God's kingdom, we serve a higher authority. When the laws of society oppose the commandments of God, we must always obey God.

Jesus has commanded us to "Go into all the world and preach the good news to all creation" (Mark 16:15). Therefore, when we don't testify about Jesus, we are disobeying God. It is our responsibility to obey this Great Commission no matter what circumstances we find ourselves in.

Talk about Jesus

The final lesson we learn from this story is that we must never stop talking about Jesus. As disciples of Christ, our number one responsibility is to tell people about Him. In our story, Peter and John were arrested because they were talking about Jesus and His resurrection from the dead. When they were asked, "By what power or what name have you healed this crippled man?" they told the Jewish leaders it was by Jesus' power and authority that the man was healed.

They constantly pointed the people to Jesus. This was because they knew that there was "no other name by which people can be saved" (4:12). Jesus is the Savior of the world (John 4:42) and the one Mediator between God and man (1 Tim. 2:5). There is no salvation apart from Him (John 14:6).

Day 8: Bold Witness Before the Jewish Leaders

We must be like the disciples. We must remain full of the Spirit, we must always obey God, and we must spend our days talking about Jesus. Right now, ask God to fill you with His Spirit, then go out and share the good news with someone you know.

Day 8: Bold Witness Before the Jewish Leaders

Day 9

A Second Outpouring in Jerusalem

Acts 4:23-37

Some Christians think, once they have been filled with the Holy Spirit, they have arrived, and there is nothing more they need to do but to bask in the blessings of God. This is foolish thinking, as our lesson today will reveal. It is the story of a second outpouring of the Spirit in Jerusalem.

Following the outpouring of the Holy Spirit on the Day of Pentecost, the church in Jerusalem became a powerful evangelistic force. The disciples witnessed with power, and God performed miracles to confirm the word. As a result, many were turning to Christ. This angered the Jewish leaders. So they arrested the apostles Peter and John and commanded them to stop preaching in Jesus' name. Then they let them go.

Peter and John returned to the company of believers and told them how the chief priests and elders had threatened them. When the believers heard this, they lifted their voices to God and began to pray with great fervor.

Day 9: A Second Jerusalem Outpouring

They prayed a powerful, God-centered missionary prayer. Rather than complain about their troubles, they acknowledged how God ruled over everything. "Sovereign Lord," they prayed, "you made the heavens and the earth and the sea, and everything else. How foolish it is for men to try to fight against you. The kings of the earth may oppose You and Your Christ, but really, they are only doing what You want them to do."

They concluded their prayer with two requests. First, they asked God for boldness to continue telling people about Jesus. Then, they asked Him to perform miraculous signs and wonders through the name of Jesus.

God answered their prayer in a dramatic way. The place where they were meeting began to shake. They knew that God had come in power. Then, just as He had done on the Day of Pentecost, the Spirit rushed inside of them and filled them all, enabling them to speak the gospel with boldness. However, they did not speak just one time. They kept on testifying about the resurrection of Jesus with power and effectiveness. Everyone could see that God's great grace was upon them.

Not only that, they were committed to one another. They were filled with godly generosity and willingly shared whatever they had. As a result, everyone's need was met. Some even sold their houses or lands and gave the money to the apostles who, in turn, shared it with those in need. One of those who did this was a man named Barnabas, a Levite from the island of Cyprus. His name means "son of encouragement."

Second Outpouring in Jerusalem

This story from Acts 4 tells of a second powerful outpouring of the Spirit on the church in Jerusalem. It is the second of seven key outpourings that occur in the Book of Acts. You will remember that the first outpouring took place on the Day of Pentecost. We will point out the other five outpourings as they occur.

For now, it is important to notice that every time the Spirit is poured out in Acts the result is powerful missional witness. That's what Jesus said would happen. In Acts 1:8 He promised His disciples, "You will receive power when the Holy Spirit comes on you; and you will be my witnesses in Jerusalem, and in all Judea and Samaria, and to the ends of the earth." This is precisely what is happening during this Second Jerusalem Outpouring.

You will remember that, after the outpouring at Pentecost, the disciples spoke in tongues. Then Peter began to proclaim Christ with power. As a result, three thousand people were saved. Now, the same thing happens after this Second Jerusalem Outpouring. Luke says, "After they prayed, the place where they were meeting was shaken. And they were all filled with the Holy Spirit and spoke the word of God boldly" (v. 31). You should commit this verse to memory.

From this story of the Second Jerusalem Outpouring, we learn four important lessons:

Once is Never Enough

First, we learn that one outpouring of the Holy Spirit is never enough. This is true for an individual seeking to minister in the power of the Spirit. It is also true for a church seeking to impact its community for Christ.

We must not make the mistake of thinking that, once we have received the Holy Spirit and spoken in tongues, we are set for life. The empowering of the Spirit must be cultivated and maintained. The work of the Holy Spirit must be experienced again and again in our lives.

Day 9: A Second Jerusalem Outpouring

On the Day of Pentecost the Spirit came powerfully on the Jerusalem church. Now, days later, God pours out His Spirit again on the church. Both times everyone present is filled. Those who had never before been filled with the Spirit were filled for the first time. Those who had been filled in the past were refilled. The result was that "they spoke the word of God with boldness" (v. 31) just as Peter had done on the Day of Pentecost.

The same is true today. God wants to pour out His Spirit on His people again and again. We must open our hearts to God and allow this to happen.

Be a People of Prayer

The second lesson we learn from this story is that, if we are going to be a people of the Spirit, we must also be a people of prayer. Throughout Acts, Luke connects the receiving of the Spirit with fervent prayer. Before Pentecost the disciples "all joined together constantly in prayer" (1:14).

Now, before the Second Jerusalem outpouring "they raised their voices together in prayer to God" (v. 24). The Jewish leaders had threatened them and commanded them "not to speak or teach at all in the name of Jesus" (v. 17). The disciples' first reaction was to pray and ask for boldness to continue witnessing.

In doing this, they were doing what Jesus had told them to do. While He was with them, He had taught them that they should repeatedly ask for the Holy Spirit (Luke 11:9-13). Now, they were simply following His instructions. They prayed, "Lord…enable your servants to speak your word with great boldness…. Stretch out your hand to heal and perform miraculous signs and wonders through the name of your holy servant Jesus" (vv. 29-30).

In Scripture, to ask God to stretch out His hand is to ask Him to manifest His presence through the power of the Holy Spirit. God answered them by sending His Spirit.

Expect to Witness

A third lesson we learn from this story is that, when we are filled with the Spirit, we should expect to witness with power. This is what happened throughout the Book of Acts. Every time the Spirit came upon someone and filled them, they began telling people about Jesus.

The pattern was first set on the Day of Pentecost. Now it is repeated. Luke says, "They were all filled with the Holy Spirit and spoke the word of God boldly" (v. 31). The subject of their witness was the story of Jesus' death and resurrection. Luke continues, "With great power the apostles continued to testify to the resurrection of the Lord Jesus, and much grace was upon them all" (v. 33).

We should expect the same today. When the Holy Spirit fills us, we should immediately look for opportunities to tell people about Jesus. And when we begin to testify, we should do so with power and boldness. Pastors must faithfully teach their people these truths.

Live Generously

A fourth and final lesson we learn from this story is that we must allow the Holy Spirit to work in our lives making us into generous people. Not only did the outpouring of the Spirit cause the disciples in Jerusalem to speak in tongues and become powerful witnesses to the lost, it further caused them to become a generous caring community. According to Luke, those who received the Spirit during this Second Jerusalem Outpouring were "one in heart and mind. No one claimed that any of his possessions was his own, but they shared everything they had" (v. 32).

Day 9: A Second Jerusalem Outpouring

You will remember that the same thing occurred after the first outpouring of the Spirit at Pentecost (2:44-45). Such Spirit-prompted generosity is essential to reaching the nations with the gospel. He is not just the Spirit of power; He is also the Spirit of love and generosity.

Day 10

A Conspiracy is Unmasked

Acts 5:1-16

He was a mighty warrior. No man could stand against him, though many had tried. Then one day, a disease was discovered inside his body. Each day the disease became stronger, and his body became weaker until, one day, the warrior died. While no man could defeat him from the outside, he was ultimately destroyed from the inside. In our story today, we learn how the devil tried to destroy the emerging church from the inside—and how his plan was foiled.

In Acts 5, the story is told of a man by the name of Ananias and his wife, Sapphira. Wanting to gain the people's admiration, the couple hatched a plot to deceive the congregation of believers. They conspired to sell a piece of property and then pretend to give the entire proceeds to the church. Secretly, however, they intended to hold back part of the sale price for themselves.

What they did not know—or did not care to know—was that Satan was working in their hearts. He was using them to infect the church with the diseases of deception and pride. In this way, he could slow the church's progress. As you will remember, the devil had first tried to stop the church by sending persecution from the outside.

Day 10: A Conspiracy is Unmasked

Since that did not work, he tried another, even more sinister, tactic. He sought to infect the church on the inside.

After selling the land, Ananias came and laid a portion of the proceeds at the apostles' feet, pretending he was giving the full price. Miraculously, the Holy Spirit revealed the couples' treachery to Peter.

Peter challenged Ananias, "How is it that Satan has filled your heart? You have lied to the Holy Spirit! The land belonged to you along with the money you made from the sale. You could have done anything you pleased with it. How could you even think of doing such a thing? You have not only lied to men but to God." God then struck Ananias, and he fell to the ground and died. Some young men carried him out and buried him.

Soon Sapphira entered the place, not knowing what had happened to her husband. She was determined to continue the deception he had started. Showing her the offering that Ananias had given, Peter asked her, "Is this the full amount you got for the land?"

"Yes," she answered, "it is the full amount."

Peter said to her, "How could you do such a thing? You agreed with your husband to test the Spirit of the Lord. Look! The men who buried your husband are at the door, and they will carry you out too."

Immediately, she fell to the ground and died. Her body was carried out and buried beside her husband's. As you can imagine, holy fear seized the whole congregation and everyone else who heard what had happened.

Because of these things, the people of Jerusalem held the disciples in high regard. They were afraid to join with them when they met together. Still, great numbers of men and women continued to believe and follow the Lord. The believers often met together in the temple under Solomon's Colonnade.

All along, the apostles continued to preach the gospel and perform miraculous signs and wonders among the people. Some people even brought their sick friends and laid them on mats beside the road. They were hoping that Peter's shadow might fall on them and they would be healed. Many came from neighboring towns bringing with them those who were sick or tormented by evil spirits. God wonderfully healed them all.

Fortified to Stand

Thus far in our study, we have witnessed three important emphases of the emerging church in Jerusalem. First, they emphasized the proclamation of the gospel. They faithfully talked about Jesus' death and resurrection to anyone who would listen.

Second, they focused on fulfilling the mission Christ had given them. He had commissioned them to be his witnesses, and they refused to veer from that mission.

Finally, they emphasized the empowering work of the Holy Spirit. They knew that they could fulfill Christ's mission only in the power of the Spirit. These themes will be repeated over and over throughout the Book of Acts. We will continue to point them out as they occur.

Not only did the Holy Spirit empower these early Christians to effectively proclaim the gospel to the lost, He fortified them to withstand persecution. He further enabled them to confront threats to the mission from within their own ranks. The duplicity of Ananias and Sapphira is one such example. Let's look at three important lessons we learn from their tragic story:

The Importance of the Mission

First, from the story of Ananias and Sapphira we learn the importance that God places on the church fulfilling its missionary mandate. If the couple's deception had been ignored, the disease would have infected others. As a result, the church would have been weakened and the mission hindered. By slaying the rebellious couple, God stopped the spread of the disease in its tracks.

While their punishment may at first glance seem severe, it demonstrates how God values His mission, and how He views those who oppose or subvert it. Paul once warned the Corinthians, "If anyone destroys God's temple [that is, the church], God will destroy him" (1 Cor. 3:17). We must never allow anything to prevent us from doing what God has commanded.

Moving in the Power of the Spirit

Second, the story of Ananias and Sapphira shows us how important it is that we learn to live and minister under the Spirit's direction. The Spirit revealed to Peter the plot of Ananias and Sapphira and how God was about to judge them. Had Peter not been walking in the Spirit, he would not have heard the Spirit's voice, and the couple's deception would have been successful. Then the door would have then been opened for the devil to work in the congregation.

Thankfully, Peter heard the voice of the Spirit, and the plan of Satan was foiled. If we are to successfully combat the enemy, we too must learn to hear and obey the Spirit's voice.

The Role of Signs and Wonders

A final lesson we learn from the story of Ananias and Sapphira is that miraculous signs and wonders play an important role in advancing God's kingdom. In our story, "the apostles performed many signs and wonders among the people" (v. 12). Those miraculous signs included healing the sick, delivering people from demonic bondage, and speaking in tongues.

When the people see God performing miracles, their hearts are opened to receive the message of the gospel. Miracles also show them God's power over Satan and His compassion for those who are suffering. In order to be used by Christ in such a way, we like the apostles, must remain full of the Spirit, open to the voice of the Spirit, and ready to act in faith.

Day 10: A Conspiracy is Unmasked

Day 11

Continued Witness in Jerusalem

Acts 5:17-41

"The blood of the martyrs is the seed of the church." So said Tertullian, the great second-century Church Father. He was pointing out how, in his day, the more the church was persecuted, the faster it grew. This is what we see happening in the Book of Acts. Because the church was Spirit-empowered and mission-focused, it grew, even in the face of persecution.

As the church in Jerusalem grew, the Jewish leaders were filled with jealousy. Again, they had the apostles arrested and thrown into public jail. During the night an angel appeared, opened the doors, and brought them out. He ordered the apostles, "Go, stand in the temple courts and tell the people about this new life in Jesus." The apostles obeyed. So, as the next morning dawned, there they were standing in the temple courts teaching people about Jesus.

When the Jewish leaders found out what was going on, they were puzzled and wondered what would happen next. They decided to send the guards to the temple to arrest the apostles. When the temple guards arrived, they seized the apostles and, once again, brought them before the Sanhedrin for questioning by the high priest.

Day 11: Continued Witness in Jerusalem

Looking the apostles in the eye, the high priest challenged them. "We gave you strict orders," he said, "not to speak any more in this name. Yet you have filled Jerusalem with your teaching." Then in a fit of anger, he blurted out, "You seem to be determined to make us guilty of killing Jesus!"

Peter was still full of the Holy Spirit, so he boldly answered the high priest, "We must obey God rather than man!" Then he began to preach the gospel to them. "You killed Jesus by hanging Him on a tree," he said, "but God raised Him up. Now God has exalted Him to His own right hand. Jesus is now the Prince and Savior. He will one day bring Israel to repentance and forgive their sins."

Peter concluded his speech with a fearless declaration: "We are witnesses of these things, and so is the Holy Spirit, whom God has given to those who obey him" (v. 32). This made the Jewish leaders so mad that they wanted to kill the apostles. They put them out for a while.

That's when one of their most respected members, a man by the name of Gamaliel, took the floor. He spoke calmly. "If these men are not from God they will surely fail," he said. "However, if God has sent them, we will find ourselves fighting against Him, and we cannot stop them." Hearing this, they called the apostles back in and flogged them. Finally, they ordered them to stop speaking in Jesus' name, then let them go.

The apostles left the Sanhedrin rejoicing. They felt honored that God had counted them worthy to suffer disgrace for the name of Jesus. And they did not stop telling people about Jesus. Day after day, in the temple courts and from house to house, they kept proclaiming the good news about Jesus the Messiah.

From this story we can learn three important lessons that can impact our ministries for Christ:

Opposition Will Come

The first lesson we learn is about how we should respond when we encounter opposition for preaching the gospel. As the church's numbers continued to increase in Jerusalem, so did the resentment of the religious authorities. Luke tells us that they were "filled with jealousy." They became so agitated that they arrested the apostles and put them in jail a second time.

Such persecution against Christians is a major theme in the Book of Acts. We can look for the same thing to happen today. Any church or disciple who faithfully proclaims the gospel can expect the devil to push back. At times, opposition may come from government authorities. At other times, it may come from envious religious leaders. When this happens, we must stay full of the Spirit and remain committed to the mission of declaring the gospel to all who will hear.

The Role of Angels

Second, from this story we learn something about the role of angels in advancing the gospel. During the night, an angel appeared and opened the doors of the jail. He told the apostles, "Go, stand in the temple courts, and tell the people all about this new life." The apostles obeyed and went into the temple and began to preach the gospel.

The ministry of angels is mentioned at least eighteen times in Acts. The writer of Hebrews describes angels as "ministering spirits sent to serve those who will inherit salvation" (1:14). Unlike Christians, angels have not been commissioned to preach the gospel. That is the job of the redeemed. However, in Acts angels do participate in advancing the kingdom of God. They do this by revealing to Christ's servants the will of God (Acts 7:38, 53, 27:23-24), by directing them in the mission (Acts 1:10-11; 8:26; 10:3-6, 22: 11:13), by comforting them in times of stress, (Acts 27:23), and by delivering them from prison (Acts 5:19; 12:7).

The angel's command to the apostles to "Go, stand, and speak" reminds us of Jesus' Great Commission where He instructs His disciples to go to all nations and preach the gospel (Matt. 28:18-20; Mark 16:15-18; Luke 24:46-48; John 20:21-22; Acts 1:8).

God's Desire to Give the Spirit

The third lesson we learn from this story is that God desires to give His Spirit to those who obey Christ's command to preach the gospel to the lost. When ordered to stop preaching in Jesus' name, Peter and the other apostles replied, "We must obey God rather than man!" He then told the Jewish authorities about Jesus. He ended his message by declaring, "We are witnesses of these things, and so is the Holy Spirit, whom God has given to those who obey him." (v. 32). (You should memorize this verse.)

In other words, God is ready to give His Spirit to anyone who will faithfully obey His command to tell others about Jesus. This promise reminds us of Jesus' earlier promise in Acts 1:8: "But you will receive power when the Holy Spirit has come upon you, and you will be my witnesses" If we will commit ourselves to preaching the gospel, God has committed himself to empowering us by His Spirit.

Day 12

A Spirit-Guided Decision

Acts 6:1-7

Someone once said, "The main thing is to keep the main thing the main thing." He was emphasizing the importance of our not allowing side issues to distract us from our primary mission. Today's story today from the Book of Acts is about how the Early Church refused to allow internal issues to distract them from their primary mission of preaching the gospel to the lost people of their city.

The church in Jerusalem continued to prosper, and each day their numbers increased. They were, however, about to face a third great challenge. As you will remember, their first challenge was persecution from the outside. This persecution came primarily from the Jewish religious authorities. Their second challenge came from within their own ranks. It was the conspiracy of Ananias and Sapphira.

Now, a third challenge arose within the community of believers—dissention among the saints. Like the first two challenges, this challenge held the potential of diverting the church from its primary mission of reaching the lost with the gospel. Just as the Holy Spirit had helped them to overcome the first two challenges, He was present to help them resolve this new one.

Day 12: A Spirit-Guided Decision

The dispute arose along racial lines. Some of the Greek-speaking Jews, known as Hellenists, complained that their widows were not being treated fairly in the daily distribution of food. They charged that the natural-born Jewish widows were being preferred above their widows. Their complaining became so intense that the apostles had to step in and manage the situation.

Directed by the Holy Spirit, the apostles developed a plan to address the issue. They said to the people, "It is not right for us to neglect the ministry of the word of God to deal with this issue. We must remain focused on prayer and the proclamation of the gospel." So they instructed the church to choose seven men "full of the Spirit and wisdom" whom they would put in charge of the matter.

The people liked their plan, so they chose seven Spirit-filled men, and the apostles appointed them to the task. As a result of this Spirit-directed action, the apostles were freed to tend to their ministry. The word of God continued to spread, and the church continued to grow.

Two of those whom the apostles appointed to care for the widows were Stephen and Philip. We will hear more about these men in upcoming lessons.

Satan's Schemes

Satan will use any tactic he can to hinder the progress of the church. Just as the devil worked in the Early Church to slow the progress of evangelism and missions, he works in the church today to do the same. However, as Paul wrote, "We are not ignorant of [Satan's] schemes" (2 Cor. 2:11). From this story, and from how the apostles handled the situation, we learn three important ministry lessons.

Stay Focused on the Mission

First, we learn that we must always stay focused on our God-given mission. We must not allow anything to cause us to turn from it. In the Jerusalem church, rapid growth brought with it misunderstanding and conflict. Luke tells us that "the Grecian Jews among them complained against the Hebraic Jews because their widows were being overlooked in the daily distribution of food" (v. 1).

This problem became a distraction to the apostles causing them to neglect the ministry to which Jesus had called them. They were determined, however, to remain focused on their primary task of preaching the gospel. They said, "It would not be right for us to neglect the ministry of the word of God in order to wait on tables" (v. 2). No, we must "give our attention to prayer and the ministry of the word" (v. 4).

Like the apostles, the primary calling of ministers of the gospel today is to seek God's face and to proclaim the message of Christ to the lost. No matter what other responsibilities they may be given, it is never right for them to neglect the ministry of the word. When this happens, they must take immediate steps to delegate the work to others so that they can remain focused on prayer and on preaching and teaching the word of God.

Choose Qualified Leaders

A second principle we learn from this story is that pastors should choose only spiritually qualified leaders to help them carry out the work of the church. The apostles told the church to choose seven men "known to be full of the Spirit and wisdom" (v. 3). They then prayed for them and laid their hands on them commissioning them to take care of the widows.

It is the responsibility of the pastor to mobilize his or her church to effectively carry out its mission of reaching the lost and discipling the saints. When they do, they must ensure that they appoint only those people who are spiritually qualified. Those they appoint must be true followers of Jesus Christ. And they must be full of the Holy Spirit and wisdom like the ones the apostles appointed in our story. If a pastor will follow these guidelines, the church will be blessed. If he does not, the church will be harmed.

Let the Spirit Lead

The third principle we learn from this story in Acts is that we must be led by the Spirit when we make decisions. The Spirit of the Lord not only empowers us to preach the gospel to the lost, He also directs us in administrating the work of the church. Church leaders must be filled with the Spirit and follow the Spirit's leadership. Then, the church will be effective in its mission of taking the gospel to the lost and planting other Spirit-empowered missionary churches.

Pastors should not try to hold their lay people back from ministry. They should rather ensure that they are filled with the Spirit, and then release them to be used by God in whatever way He may choose.

As a result of the apostles' Spirit-directed decision to appoint seven "deacons" to help them in the work, the word of the Lord continued to spread in Jerusalem. Luke says that "the number of disciples in Jerusalem increased rapidly, and a large number of priests became obedient to the faith" (v. 7).

Day 13

Stephen's Spirit-Empowered Witness and Death

Acts 6:8-8:1a

Have you ever had someone tell a lie about you? How did you react? In the story of Stephen, we learn how he responded when evil people told lies about him. Yet, they did more than just tell lies about him. They cursed him to his face, dragged him out of the city, and stoned him to death. He responded by sharing Christ with them and praying for them.

You will remember that Stephen was one of the seven "deacons" chosen by the people to care for the widows in the Jerusalem church. Because he was full of God's grace and empowered by the Holy Spirit, he "did great wonders and miraculous signs among the people" (v. 8). Stephen's good works, however, angered the radical members of the Synagogue of the Freedmen in Jerusalem.

One day, these men approached Stephen and began to argue with him. However, they were embarrassed because they could not stand against his wisdom. He was speaking words that the Holy Spirit was giving him. So they persuaded some men to lie to the temple

Day 13: Stephen's Spirit-Empowered Witness and Death

authorities and say, "We have heard Stephen speak words of blasphemy against Moses and against God" (6:11).

Hearing this, the authorities seized Stephen and brought him before the Sanhedrin. There they produced false witnesses who lied about Stephen, saying that he was blaspheming the temple and the Law of Moses. They claimed Stephen had said that Jesus would destroy the temple and change the laws of God. Even as they were speaking, everyone's head turned toward Stephen. They were amazed because his face was shining like the face of an angel.

The high priest asked Stephen, "Are these charges true?" Again, Stephen spoke by the Spirit. He told the Jewish leaders how God had called and led their father Abraham. He spoke of how God had blessed his descendants and how, through Moses, God had delivered the children of Israel from Egyptian bondage. Just as the children of Israel had rejected Moses whom God sent to them, they were now rejecting Jesus.

Then Stephen accused them. "You stiff-necked people," he said, "you are just like your fathers. You have always resisted the Holy Spirit, and now you have murdered Jesus, the very one whom God sent to save you" (v. 51).

This infuriated his accusers. They became so enraged that they began to grind their teeth at Stephen. He, however, was full of the Spirit. He looked up to heaven and saw God's glory, and Jesus standing at the right hand of the Father. He then cried out, "Look, I see heaven open and the Son of Man standing at the right hand of God!" (v. 56).

This so enraged Stephen's accusers that they covered their ears and began to shout at the top of their voices. They then dragged him out of the city and began to stone him. As the stones pelted Stephen's

Day 13: Stephen's Spirit-Empowered Witness and Death

body, he prayed, "Lord, do not hold this sin against them." Then he uttered a final prayer, "Lord Jesus, receive my spirit," and died. Those who took part in the murder of Stephen laid their coats at the feet of a young Jewish Pharisee named Saul of Tarsus who was consenting to Stephen's death. We will hear more about Saul in future lessons.

From this amazing story about Stephen, we learn three important lessons about how we should respond when people lie about us and seek to harm us for preaching the gospel.

Remain Full of the Spirit

First, we learn that we should remain full of the Spirit. Like many of us, Stephen had been baptized in the Holy Spirit. More importantly, he remained full of the Spirit. Then, when he faced danger, the Spirit came to his aid. Jesus had promised, "When you are brought before synagogues, rulers and authorities, do not worry about how you will defend yourselves or what you will say, for the Holy Spirit will teach you at that time what you should say" (Luke 12:11-12). The Spirit was now fulfilling Jesus' promise.

Like Stephen, we too must remain full of the Spirit at all times. If we will do this, we can be sure that the Spirit will strengthen us in our times of need. As Stephen was dying, the Holy Spirit gave him a heavenly vision. "Look," he said, "I see heaven open and the Son of Man standing at the right hand of God" (v. 56). We can remain full of the Spirit by being committed to Christ's mission, living holy lives, and praying often in the Holy Spirit.

Share the Gospel

Second, from the story of Stephen we learn that we should always share the gospel, even in the face of danger. Stephen believed that it was more important to declare the message of Christ than to preserve his own life.

On occasions, God calls upon us to preach Christ in uncomfortable and dangerous situations. At such times, we must never compromise the gospel message. We must, like Stephen, be bold and always "speak the truth in love" (Eph. 4:15).

At such times, we must know that Christ will be with us, just as He was with Stephen. Jesus has promised, "Surely I am with you always, to the very end of the age" (Matt. 28:20). He also said, "I will never leave you nor forsake you" (Heb. 13:5). Just as Jesus honored Stephen in his death, He will honor us—if we will remain faithful unto Him. Remember Jesus' words: "Be faithful until death, and I will give you the crown of life" (Rev. 2:10, NKJV).

Show the Love of Christ

Finally, from the story of Stephen we learn that we must always show the love of Christ, even when people attack and abuse us. Stephen died as Jesus died. Both were full of the Holy Spirit (see Heb. 9:14), and both showed love for those who were killing them. Just as Jesus prayed for his murderers, Stephen prayed for his: "He fell on his knees and cried out, 'Lord, do not hold this sin against them'" (v. 60).

Stephen not only bore witness to Christ in his life, he bore faithful witness in his death. Jesus has taught us, "Love your enemies and pray for those who persecute you" (Matt. 5:44). We can do this if we will remain full of the Holy Spirit. The Bible says, "God has poured out his love into our hearts by the Holy Spirit, whom he has given us" (Rom. 5:5).

Day 14

Philip's Powerful Ministry in Samaria

Acts 8:1-13

Have you ever stamped your foot on a burning fire? What happened? The embers scattered in all directions. If you were not careful, they could even have started other fires. This is a picture of what happened to the church in Jerusalem.

Using Saul of Tarsus and others, the devil tried to stamp out the fires of evangelism that had been kindled on the Day of Pentecost. The Bible says, "On that day [the day Stephen was stoned] a great persecution broke out against the church at Jerusalem" (v. 1). However, the devil's plan did not work. The persecution only scattered the flame of the gospel into new areas. One of those areas was a city in Samaria.

Jesus had said that His disciples were to be His Spirit-empowered witnesses "in Jerusalem, and in all Judea and Samaria, and to the ends of the earth" (Acts 1:8). However, up to now, the church had been proclaiming the message of Christ in and around the city of Jerusalem only. The time had come for the church to move out into Judea and Samaria.

Day 14: Philip's Powerful Ministry in Samaria

On the same day Stephen was stoned, more persecution came against the church in Jerusalem. This violent rampage was led by Saul of Tarsus. He began moving from house to house, arresting Christians and throwing them into prison. And he was there lending his support when others were put to death.

As a result of this persecution, many believers fled for their lives into the nearby regions of Judea and Samaria. Amazingly, everywhere they went, they preached the gospel. The apostles, however, remained in Jerusalem, enduring the full brunt of the persecution.

Philip, one of the seven Spirit-filled brothers chosen to care for the widows, went to a city in nearby Samaria. There he began telling everyone about Jesus. Miraculous signs accompanied his preaching. Through the power of the Spirit cripples were healed, and with shrieks impure spirits came out of many.

Great crowds gathered to see the miracles and listen to what Philip had to say. Many believed Philip's message about the good news of the kingdom of God and the name of Jesus. They were all baptized in water. As a result of this revival, great joy came to the city.

One of those who was baptized was a sorcerer by the name of Simon. For a long time he had amazed the people with his magical powers, so much so that they called him the "Great Power of God." Simon was impressed by the incredible signs that followed Philip's preaching, so he began to follow Philip everywhere he went. (We will learn more about Simon in our next lesson.)

A Major Step Forward

This scattering of believers from Jerusalem represents a major step forward in the church's development from a regional Jewish sect into a universal body of believers. It launched the church's first venture into non-purely-Jewish missions. It thus challenged the long-held prejudices that Jewish Christians had brought into the church from their religious and cultural past.

We learn three important lessons from this story:

Witness Everywhere

First, we learn that everywhere we go, no matter what the circumstances, we should witness for Christ. Luke says that the scattered Jerusalem Christians "preached the word wherever they went" (v. 4). But what gave these persecuted Christians such zeal and boldness? The answer is, they were filled with the Spirit and fully committed to God's mission.

Although we do not welcome persecution, sometimes it will come, especially if we are faithful to proclaim the message of Christ. When persecution does come, we must be ready. We can do this if we, like those first Christians in Jerusalem, will stay focused on Christ's mission and remain full of the Holy Spirit.

Expect Miracles

The second lesson we learn from this story of Philip's ministry in Samaria is that, if we will go and faithfully preach the gospel, we can expect God to confirm His word with miraculous signs. After commanding us to "go into all the world and preach the good news to all creation," Jesus promised, "and these signs will accompany those who believe: In my name they will drive out demons...they will place their hands on sick people, and they will get well" (Mark 16:15-17).

This is what happened with Philip. His Spirit-inspired proclamation was accompanied by powerful Spirit-generated signs. After seeing these signs, the crowds listened more closely to what Philip said.

True gospel preaching always involves both powerful proclamation of the gospel (known as "truth encounters") and mighty demonstrations of kingdom power (known as "power encounters"). We must always be faithful to preach the message in the power of the Holy Spirit. If we will do this, we can expect God to confirm His word through miraculous signs and wonders.

Baptize New Believers

The final lesson we learn from this story is that soon after new believers commit their lives to Christ, they should be baptized in water. Luke wrote, "But when they believed Philip as he preached the good news of the kingdom of God and the name of Jesus Christ, they were baptized, both men and women" (v. 12). Philip was following the instructions of Jesus to His disciples. In the Great Commission He commanded them to "go and make disciples of all nations, baptizing them in the name of the Father and of the Son and of the Holy Spirit" (Matt. 28:19).

New believers should be baptized in water soon after they commit their lives to Christ. This crucial act of obedience is an essential part of their following Him. It is a testimony to the world that they have died with Christ and have been raised with Him to new life. It is further a public declaration that they have committed themselves to His mission of redeeming the nations.

Day 15

The Samaritan Outpouring

Acts 8:14-25

Sometimes people achieve more than we expect. This was the case with Philip, one of the seven brothers who had been chosen to take care of the widows in the Jerusalem church. As a result of an outbreak of violent persecution in the city, he and many other Christians fled for their lives into the surrounding regions. The apostles, however, remained in Jerusalem.

Then one day a messenger arrived in Jerusalem from Samaria. He found the place where the apostles were staying and told them of a great revival that had broken out in the city.

The messenger described how Philip had gone to Samaria. When he arrived, he began to boldly proclaim Christ to the city's residents. God confirmed his message by healing the sick and crippled and by setting people free from demonic bondages. As a result of Philip's ministry, hundreds of Samaritans had accepted the word of the Lord and were baptized in water.

The apostles must have rejoiced as they listened to this wonderful report. However, as they inquired further, they realized that there was a crucial missing ingredient in the Samaritan revival. Alarmingly, no one was being baptized in the Holy Spirit. Although all who belong to Christ are indwelt by the Spirit, these new believers had not yet been baptized in the Holy Spirit and empowered as Christ's witnesses. In the apostles' minds, this was a grave omission.

Had not Jesus commanded His disciples to stay in Jerusalem, and wait for the gift of the Holy Spirit? And had He not promised them, "You will receive power when the Holy Spirit comes on you; and you will be my witnesses in Jerusalem, and in all Judea and Samaria, and to the ends of the earth"? (Acts 1:8).

The apostles knew that Jesus' command and promise applied to the Samaritans every bit as much as it did to them. In fact, the Lord's command to be empowered by the Spirit was for all of God's people until the gospel had been proclaimed to the ends of the earth and Jesus had returned from heaven. Now, if the Samaritans were to fully participate in God's mission, they too would need to be empowered by the Spirit.

The gospel must not only go *to* Samaria, it must go *from* Samaria to the ends of the earth. Because of this, the apostles sent Peter and John to Samaria to pray for the new Christians there to receive the Holy Spirit.

When Peter and John arrived in the city, they called together all who had been saved. After instructing them, they began laying their hands on them. As they did, these new Samaritan believers were filled with the Holy Spirit, just as the Jewish believers had been on the Day of Pentecost.

You will remember from our last lesson that one of those whom Philip had baptized in water was Simon, who had been a sorcerer. This man was captivated by what happened as believers were being filled with the Spirit. While the Bible does not say what so intrigued

Day 15: The Samaritan Outpouring

him, he likely heard them speaking in tongues just as the 120 had done on the Day of Pentecost. Simon offered to pay the apostles money if they would give him the power to lay hands on people, causing them to receive the Spirit.

On hearing this, Peter became angry. He rebuked Simon saying, "May your money perish with you. Don't you know that you cannot buy the gift of God with money?" He then looked Simon in the eye and said, "Repent of this wickedness and ask the Lord to forgive you and deliver you from your greediness. You are full of bitterness and captive to sin."

On hearing this, Simon became frightened, and begged Peter, "Pray for me that this will not happen to me."

After these things, the apostles spent several days in Samaria teaching and proclaiming the good news. They were so inspired that, as they returned to Jerusalem, they preached the gospel in several Samaritan villages. This was the first time they had preached the gospel to anyone other than pure Jews.

From the story of the Samaritan Outpouring, we can glean four important missionary insights:

Power for Witness

The first missionary insight we gain from our story is that, in order to become effective witnesses for Christ, we must all be empowered by the Holy Spirit. We have already encountered this lesson in our study. And it is a lesson that we will encounter again as we proceed through Acts. We must not miss this all-important lesson Luke is trying to teach us.

The Samaritan Outpouring is the third key outpouring of the Spirit to occur in the Book of Acts. As you may recall, the first

Day 15: The Samaritan Outpouring

outpouring occurred at Pentecost. The second also occurred in Jerusalem a few days later. Now, a third outpouring occurs in Samaria. Each of these three outpourings resulted in powerful missional witness and each demonstrates the empowerment-witness motif that is repeated throughout Acts. The Samaritan Outpouring is yet is another fulfillment of Jesus' promise in Acts 1:8: "But you will receive power when the Holy Spirit comes on you; and you will be my witnesses…"

To and From

The second missionary insight we gain from the story of the Samaritan Outpouring is that everywhere the gospel goes *to,* it must go *from*. The apostles understood this truth. That is why they were so intent on praying with the Samaritans to receive the Holy Spirit. According to Jesus' plan in Acts 1:8, the gospel was to go to Samaria, but it was not to stop there. And if the gospel was to go from Samaria, the new Samaritan church would need to be empowered by the Holy Spirit.

As a result of the Samaritans' receiving the Spirit, a new center of missions endeavor was created. Luke tells us that "the church throughout Judea, Galilee and Samaria…was strengthened; and encouraged by the Holy Spirit, it grew in numbers" (Acts 9:31). We must never be content knowing that the gospel has come to our place. We must commit ourselves to taking the gospel to other villages and communities.

God Can Use Anyone

A third important missionary insight we gain from the story of the Samaritan Outpouring is that God can use anyone who will be filled with the Spirit and fully commit themselves to His mission. The Samaritans were a mixed-race people. They were part Jew and part

Gentile. Because of this, the Jews despised them. They accused the Samaritans of perverting the true religion of God.

However, by filling these new Samaritan believers with the Holy Spirit, God was showing that He had accepted them as full participants in His mission. Not only will God save anybody from any tribe or religion who will repent of his or her sins and trust Christ, He will also fill them with His Spirit and empower them to share the gospel with others.

Not For Sale

A final insight we gain from this story is that the power and blessings of God cannot be bought and sold. Simon made two serious miscalculations. First, he assumed that Peter and John were able to give the Holy Spirit to the people they prayed for. However, no man has ever had that power, and no man ever will. Only God can give people the Holy Spirit.

The second miscalculation Simon made was in thinking that the power and blessing of God could be bought and sold with money. He was wrong again. The power and blessings of God cannot be bought or sold. However, God will freely give both to those who will fully commit themselves to Him and His mission.

Day 15: The Samaritan Outpouring

Day 16

Philip's Spirit-Directed Ministry in Gaza

Acts 8:26-40

God sometimes asks us to do things that do not seem to make sense. That's because God sees the big picture and we see only a small part of it. In our story today, God asked Philip to do something that, at first glance, did not seem to make sense.

Following the outpouring of the Spirit in Samaria, the revival intensified. That's when God did something that may have puzzled many of the disciples there. In the midst of this powerful move of the Spirit, an angel appeared to Philip and told him to leave the revival and go south to the desert road that goes down from Jerusalem to Gaza, a distance of about 50 miles (80 kilometers). Philip obeyed and went.

On his way, he met an Ethiopian nobleman riding in a chariot. This was no chance encounter. God had arranged this meeting between Philip and this high governmental official in the court of Candace, the queen of Ethiopia. The man was returning home from a pilgrimage to Jerusalem to worship at the temple there. As he went, he was reading aloud from the passage in the book of Isaiah that says,

Day 16: Philip's Spirit-Directed Ministry in Gaza

"He was led like a sheep to the slaughter, and as a lamb before the shearer is silent, so he did not open his mouth" (v. 32; Isa. 53:7).

That's when the Spirit of God told Philip, "Go to that chariot and stay near it." So Philip ran up to the chariot. Hearing the Ethiopian's words, he asked the man, "Do you understand what you are reading?"

The Ethiopian replied, "How can I, unless someone explains it to me. Tell me, who is the prophet talking about, himself or someone else?" He then invited Philip to come up into the chariot and sit with him. Philip preached to him the good news about Jesus from the very passage the man was reading.

Soon they came to a body of water. So the man said to Philip, "Look! Here is water. Why shouldn't I be baptized immediately?"

Philip answered, "You can, if you truly believe that Jesus is the Son of God." The man responded, "I believe!" At that, they both went down into the water, and Philip baptized him. Immediately the Spirit of the Lord whisked Philip away, and the eunuch continued on his journey rejoicing.

The next time Philip was seen, he was in Azotus, a Philistine city about 20 miles (32 kilometers) to the north of Gaza. He continued his journey northward along the coastline preaching the gospel in all the towns until he arrived in Caesarea.

The Ends of the Earth

In Acts 1:8, Jesus said that His disciples would be His witnesses "to the ends of the earth." In the ancient world, the term Ethiopia referred to all of Africa south of Egypt. The word literally means "people with dark skin." Ethiopia at that time represented the ends of the earth to the south. In Acts, the Ethiopian nobleman is the first pure Gentile to receive the gospel.

Superintendent of the Harvest

The story of Philip's witness to the Ethiopian is an example of how the Holy Spirit acts as "Superintendent of the Harvest." As such, He guides and directs the work of the church. In our story, He tells Philip where to go and what to say. In future lessons, we will see the Holy Spirit directing the harvest in various ways.

From this account of Philip's ministry on the road to Gaza, we learn three important lessons:

God's Concern for All

First, we learn that God is concerned about all people from all nations and tribes. Philip first preached the gospel to the Samaritans, a mixed-race people who were part Jew and part Gentile. Now the Spirit sends him to share Christ with an African man who was pure Gentile. God wants all people to know about His Son, Jesus.

In sharing the good news with a Gentile man, Philip was following the example of Jesus who himself often ministered to non-Jews. Further, the Book of Acts often speaks of those who ministered to people of different tribes and nationalities.

We should do the same today. Jehovah God is the God of all nations and peoples and He loves all people equally. We must therefore commit ourselves to taking the gospel to people of all nations and tribes.

Divine Appointments

The second lesson we learn from Philip's ministry on the road to Gaza is that God often arranges for us "divine appointments"—and He expects us to keep them. A divine appointment is a witnessing opportunity arranged by God himself.

Day 16: Philip's Spirit-Directed Ministry in Gaza

This is what happened in our story. God divinely set up the meeting between Philip and the Ethiopian nobleman. He then oversaw the timing and circumstances of the encounter. Finally, the Spirit directed Philip into the witnessing event. As a result, Philip was able to present the gospel with maximum effect.

However, had Philip not been able to hear the Spirit's voice, he would have missed his appointment. How many divine appointments have we missed because we were not listening to the voice of the Spirit? We must know how to recognize His voice when He speaks to us. We can learn to hear God's voice if we will walk in the Spirit and live prayerful lives. When the Spirit does speak, we must be quick to obey.

Talk about Jesus

A third lesson we learn from Philip's ministry on the road to Gaza is that we must always be quick to tell others about Jesus. When Philip heard the Ethiopian reading from the book of Isaiah, he asked him, "Do you understand what you are reading?" The Ethiopian answered, "How can I unless someone helps me to understand?" At that, Philip climbed into his chariot, and from the very passage he was reading, told him the good news about Jesus.

We should do the same. We must use every chance we get to tell people about Jesus. He is the only one who can save them. Remember Peter's words, "Salvation is found in no one else, for there is no other name under heaven given to men by which we must be saved" (Acts 4:12). Christians who spend all of their time talking about other less important things make a serious mistake. Jesus must remain the central focus of all our teaching and preaching.

Day 17

Saul Meets Jesus

Acts 9:1-9

When I met Christ, my life was changed. I was a wild and willful young man who cared little about anything but himself. Then I met Christ, and He turned my life around. However, my story is not that unusual. Millions throughout the world can testify of how Christ transformed their lives too. Today's story from the Book of Acts tells the dramatic story of how Saul of Tarsus encountered Jesus of Nazareth, and how his life was forever changed.

While Philip was ministering in Samaria and western Judea, Saul was back in Jerusalem lashing out against the Christians there. Day after day he was "breathing out murderous threats against the Lord's disciples" (v. 1). He went from house to house, arresting believers, and putting them into prison. He tried to get them to renounce their faith in Christ. That's when he received word that the church had spread into Damascus, the capital city of Syria.

Damascus was about 150 miles (250 kilometers)—or four to six days travel—to the north of Jerusalem. Saul thought to himself, *This plague must be stopped!* So he went to the high priest and got permission to arrest any Christian he found in Damascus, man or woman, and bring them back to Jerusalem as prisoners. Soon Saul and his gang were on their way to Damascus. After several days travel, the city was finally in sight.

That's when it happened! Suddenly Jesus appeared to them in a blinding flash of light. Dazed, Saul fell to the ground. Then the Lord Jesus spoke to him out of the light. "Saul, Saul," He asked, "Why are you persecuting me?"

Saul replied, "Who are you, Lord?"

Jesus answered, "I am Jesus, whom you are persecuting. Now get up and go into the city. There, you will be told what to do."

The men who were with Saul heard a loud sound; however, they did not understand the words that Jesus spoke to him. Because Saul had been blinded by the intense light, his men had to lead him by the hand into the city. For the next three days he had nothing to eat or drink.

Saul Encounters Christ

This is the third time we meet Saul in the Book of Acts. We first met him in Acts 7. There we saw him giving encouragement to the men who murdered Stephen. Then, in chapter 8 we watched as he began to violently persecute the church in Jerusalem, scattering the believers throughout Judea and Samaria.

In today's story, Saul's rampage against the church continues. He heads off to Damascus to terrorize the Christians there, just as he had done in Jerusalem. Little did he know that an encounter with the living Christ would dramatically change the direction of his life.

The bright light that Saul saw came from the resurrected Jesus. This is the same Jesus whom Stephen saw standing at the right hand of God. It was from this exalted position that Jesus had poured out the Holy Spirit on the Day of Pentecost (2:33). Now in His glorified body, Jesus appears to Saul—and His glory shines through like the noonday sun.

Saul is Saved

At this moment, Saul was saved. We know this because he called Jesus "Lord" and submitted himself completely to Christ's will. Later, when he meets Ananias, this disciple from Damascus calls him "Brother Saul." In our next lesson, we will learn how Saul is later filled with the Holy Spirit. Because of this, we know that salvation and the baptism in the Holy Spirit are two separate experiences. When one is saved, his or her sins are forgiven and they are made a part of God's family. When one is baptized in the Holy Spirit, they are empowered to take the message of salvation to others.

We learn three important lessons from the story of Saul's encounter with Jesus on the road to Damascus:

Christ Loves the Church

First, we learn how very much Jesus loves His church. On the Damascus Road, Jesus asked Saul, "Why are you persecuting me?" By persecuting the church, Saul was persecuting Christ. This shows how closely Jesus identifies with His church. In his letter to the Ephesians, Paul wrote that Jesus loved the church so much that He died for it (Eph. 5:25). Paul often referred to the church as the "body of Christ."

If Jesus loves the church, then so should we. The church is Christ's means of taking the message of salvation to a lost world. We should do everything we can to support and promote the church.

God Can Save Anyone

The second lesson we learn from this story is that God's grace can redeem anyone. When Saul met Christ, Satan was using him to oppose the work of God and destroy the church. In the minds of many Christians, he was the least likely person in all Israel to turn to Christ.

Nevertheless, God had a plan for his life. He was able to see into Saul's heart and know how much he really wanted to serve God. So Jesus appeared to Saul and revealed himself to him. When Saul saw the resurrected Christ, he gave himself completely to the Savoir.

We should never lose hope, saying that a person is too far from God to be saved. We must rather pray for them and share Christ's love with them. By God's grace they too can become faithful followers of Jesus Christ. In our eyes it may seem impossible, but with God all things are possible.

Lives Can Be Changed

A third lesson we learn from the story of Saul's conversion is how a person's life can be changed by an encounter with Christ. When Saul met Jesus on the Damascus road, an inner change took place. In a moment, the church's great persecutor became its devoted promoter.

Jesus called this experience being "born again" (John 3:7). When a person is born again, he or she becomes a "new creation" in Christ. Truly, "the old has gone [and] the new is here" (2 Cor. 5:17). To be born again one must repent of their sins and put his or her faith in Christ alone for salvation. They must then take up their cross daily and follow Christ. Have you committed your life to Christ? Would you do it right now?

Day 18

Saul is Empowered by the Holy Spirit

Acts 9:10-30

Mbewe lived in a village in northern Malawi, Africa. He had been following Christ for several years, and was a faithful elder in the local Assemblies of God church. However, in all those years, he had never led even one person to Christ. He had wanted to, but he was afraid to try. Then one Sunday morning his pastor preached a message on the baptism in the Holy Spirit. He told of how, in the Book of Acts, when people were filled with the Spirit, they became bold witnesses for Christ. Mbewe longed for such boldness.

When the pastor asked who wanted to be filled with the Spirit, Mbewe went to the front of the church. During the prayer time, he opened his heart to God and simply asked Jesus to fill him with the Holy Spirit. The Holy Spirit came upon him, and he was filled with the Spirit. As the power of God flowed through his being, he began to speak in other tongues.

After that, Mbewe began to witness with boldness. In a short time he had led several people to Christ. He now leads the outreach

Day 18: Saul is Empowered by the Holy Spirit

ministry in his church. In the past few years he has helped to plant four churches in surrounding villages.

Today's story from the Book of Acts is similar to Mbewe's story. In it, Saul of Tarsus is filled with the Spirit and becomes a powerful witness for Christ.

You will remember from our last lesson that, as Saul and his band approached the city of Damascus, Jesus appeared to him in a bright light. As a result, Saul was blinded, and his traveling companions had to lead him by the hand into the city. They took him to the house of Judas located on Straight Street.

Also living in Damascus was a certain disciple named Ananias. The Lord Jesus appeared to him in a vision. He told Ananias to go to Judas' house and pray for Saul that his eyes might be given back their sight.

Ananias had heard the reports about Saul's persecution of the church in Jerusalem, and he knew Saul had come to Damascus to do the same there. He was therefore reluctant to obey the Lord, and he told the Lord so.

But the Lord commanded Ananias, "Go! I have chosen this man to proclaim my name to the Gentiles and their kings and before the people of Israel." The Lord further told Ananias that He would fill Saul with the Holy Spirit. Ananias obeyed and went.

When Ananias arrived at the house, he found Saul in prayer. He greeted Saul and told him why he had come. Ananias then laid his hands on Saul and prayed for him. Immediately what appeared to be scales fell from Saul's eyes, and he could see again. What's more, he was filled with the Holy Spirit. Saul then got up and was baptized. Afterward, he ate some food and regained his strength.

Day 18: Saul is Empowered by the Holy Spirit

Paul's being filled with the Spirit resulted in his becoming a powerful witness for Christ in Damascus, just as the disciples' filling at Pentecost had resulted in their becoming powerful witnesses in Jerusalem. Immediately Saul began to tell everyone that Jesus was the Son of God.

At first, the Christians in Damascus distrusted him because of his reputation. Nevertheless, he kept on preaching and teaching the people that Jesus was truly the Messiah. This went on for quite a while. Then some Jews decided to kill him. So one night he escaped over the wall of the city and headed for Jerusalem.

When he arrived in Jerusalem, he tried to join the disciples there, but they too were afraid of him. That's when Barnabas befriended him and introduced him to the apostles. He told them about how Saul had met Jesus on the Damascus Road and how for some time he had been fearlessly telling others about Christ.

Paul then began moving throughout Jerusalem preaching the message of Jesus. However, some Greek-speaking Jews began to plot to murder him, just as they had murdered Stephen. Because of this, his friends whisked Paul away and took him to the coastal city of Caesarea. From there he set sail for Tarsus.

The Damascus Outpouring

Saul's receiving the Holy Spirit is the fourth key outpouring of the Holy Spirit in the Book of Acts. Because it happened in Damascus, it is called the Damascus Outpouring. The other three, which we have already looked at, are

- the Day of Pentecost (Acts 2:1-4),
- the Second Jerusalem Outpouring (Acts 4:31),
- and the Samaritan Outpouring (Acts 8:15-17).

Day 18: Saul is Empowered by the Holy Spirit

As with the previous three outpourings, the Damascus Outpouring resulted in Spirit-empowered witness. Upon being filled with the Spirit, Saul "at once...began to preach in the synagogues that Jesus is the Son of God" (v. 20).

This is another example of the empowerment-witness motif found throughout Acts. Luke is clearly trying to teach us something. He wants us to know that it is essential for every believer to be empowered by the Spirit in order to become an effective witness for Christ.

Some have wondered, *Did Saul speak in tongues when Ananias laid hands on him to receive the Holy Spirit?* Although the text does not say, there is strong evidence that he did. For he would later write to the Christians in Corinth telling them, "I thank God that I speak in tongues more than all of you" (1 Cor. 14:18). Also, later on in the Book of Acts, when Paul lays his hands on the disciples in Ephesus, "they spoke in tongues and prophesied" (Acts 19:6).

We can expect the same thing to happen today. When believers are filled with the Holy Spirit, they will speak in tongues as the Spirit gives utterance, just as those first disciples did on the Day of Pentecost (2:4). Then, like Paul and others throughout the Book of Acts, they will go out and tell others that Jesus is the Son of God.

Saul's conversion and subsequent empowering by the Spirit is one of the most significant events in history. Had he not been saved, and had he not been filled with the Spirit, we would not have the thirteen books he wrote, which make up about one-third of our New Testament. As a result, our understanding of Christ and His redemptive work would be greatly diminished.

Furthermore, the Early Church would have had no apostle to the Gentiles as we read about in the last sixteen chapters of the Book of

Acts. The world would look much different today if Saul had not been saved and empowered by the Holy Spirit.

We learn two important lessons from the account of Saul's being filled with the Holy Spirit:

The Importance of Being Empowered

First, we learn the importance of being empowered by the Spirit in order to be effective witnesses for Christ. We have emphasized this lesson already in our study. However, because in Acts Luke chooses to emphasize it again and again, we will do the same. In this story, Jesus was so intent on Saul receiving the Spirit that He appeared to Ananias in a vision and told him to go pray with Saul. Once Saul received the Spirit, he immediately began to witness for Christ.

God Can Use Anyone

A second lesson we learn from this story is that God can use anyone who will be filled with the Spirit and obedient to His voice. One does not have to be an apostle or preacher to be used by God. The Bible calls Ananias a "certain disciple." He was probably a layman in the Damascus church. However, he was full of the Spirit and committed to God's mission, so God was able to use him.

Though we never read of him again in the Book of Acts, this simple man overcame his fear and helped to change the course of history. He was used by God to lead the great apostle to the Gentiles into the baptism in the Holy Spirit. The same is true today, God will use anyone who will be empowered by the Holy Spirit and remain committed to Him and His mission.

Day 18: Saul is Empowered by the Holy Spirit

Day 19

Peter Ministers in Judea

Acts 9:31-43

First century citizens had no radios or televisions, and certainly no cellphones. For the most part, news spread by word of mouth. Sometimes it spread slowly; at other times, it spread more quickly. The news about Saul's conversion must have spread especially fast. The ringleader of the persecution against the church had been saved!

After Saul's conversion, things calmed down for the saints throughout Judea, Galilee, and Samaria. Because of this, the apostles in Jerusalem were able to move about more freely. So Peter decided to tour western Judea and check on the saints there. Leaving Jerusalem, he went about 26 miles (42 kilometers) northwest to the town of Lydda. When he arrived, he was taken to the bedside of a man named Aeneas. The man was crippled and had been bedridden for eight long years.

Peter addressed the man. "Aeneas," he said, "Jesus Christ heals you!" Then, looking him in the eye, Peter ordered him, "Get up and roll up your mat." Immediately Aeneas jumped to his feet and began to walk. Everyone who saw this miracle was amazed.

Day 19: Peter Ministers in Judea

About that time, two messengers arrived from the nearby seaport of Joppa. "Please come at once," they begged Peter, "our dear friend Tabitha is very sick, at the point of death." Peter immediately set off for Joppa.

Now Tabitha was a wonderful Christian woman. Some people referred to her as Dorcas, which means "gazelle" in the local language. She was known for her good deeds and how she was always helping the poor.

When Peter arrived in Joppa, he received the sad news that the beloved Tabitha had died. Peter responded, "Take me to her."

When he arrived at the upstairs room where she had been laid, he found her body surrounded by some widows whom she had cared for. With sobs they showed Peter the robes and other clothes she had made for them. Peter asked them to leave him alone in the room with the body.

After they had left, he knelt and prayed. He then spoke directly to the dead woman, commanding her, "Tabitha, get up!" Amazingly, she opened her eyes, looked at Peter, and sat up. Peter then took her by the hand and helped her to stand. When he presented her alive to the people, they all rejoiced at what God had done. This great miracle became known all over Joppa. Many people came to the Lord as a result.

Jesus the Healer

Peter's Judean ministry shows us that the apostles not only evangelized the lost; they also ministered to the needs of the believers. However, even their pastoral care for the people had evangelistic implications. When outsiders observed the Lord's goodness toward His people, many sinners turned to Christ.

Day 19: Peter Ministers in Judea

Peter' words to Aeneas, "Jesus Christ heals you," reminds us that Jesus is the healer. Even when Christ uses one of His ministers to heal the sick, we must never forget that the healing comes from Christ not from any person. Peter's words tell us that, even after His ascension into heaven, Jesus continued His healing ministry on earth. Before Jesus returned to heaven He promised His disciples, "Surely, I am with you always, to the very end of the age" (Matt. 28:20). Truly, "Jesus Christ is the same yesterday, today and forever" (Heb. 13:8).

From the account of Peter's ministry in western Judea, we learn three important ministry lessons:

Stay Full of the Spirit

First, we learn that we, like Peter, must at all times remain full of the Spirit and open to His directions. Peter was first filled with the Spirit on the Day of Pentecost. He then preached a powerful Spirit-anointed message and three thousand people were saved. Now several years later, Peter is still ministering in the power of the Holy Spirit. How did he know that Jesus wanted to raise Aeneas from his sickbed and Tabitha from the dead? He knew these things because he was full of the Holy Spirit and able to hear His voice.

Jesus once explained why He healed a certain crippled man. "The Son can do nothing by himself," He explained, "he can do only what he sees his Father doing" (John 5:19). In other words, Jesus always listened to His Father and did what the Father told Him to do.

This same thing happened with Peter. He heard the voice of the Spirit telling him what to do. Because of this, he was able to say to Aeneas, "Jesus Christ heals you." Later, he was able to raise Tabitha from the dead because the Spirit had revealed to him that it was God's will to do so. We, like Peter, must learn to minister in the Spirit's power and under the Spirit's guidance. Only then will we be truly effective in our ministries.

Imitate Jesus

The second lesson we learn from Peter's ministry in western Judea is that we are to imitate the ministry of Jesus. Peter's ministry in the region was in many ways an imitation of Jesus' ministry. Jesus always ministered in the Spirit's power and under the Spirit's guidance. He often healed people through the spoken word.

Peter did these same things. In commanding Aeneas and Tabitha to "get up," Peter was following the example of Jesus who commanded the leper to "be clean" (Matt. 8:2) and the man with a shriveled hand to "stretch out your hand" (Matt. 12:13). Like Jesus, Peter also ensured that those he ministered to heard the gospel. As a result, many people turned to the Lord. As ministers of the gospel, we too should also seek to imitate the ministry of Jesus, both in word and action.

The Purpose of Miracles

A third lesson we learn from this story concerns the twofold purpose of miracles. The first reason God performs miracles is to demonstrate His love for people. Jesus often healed sick people because He had compassion on their suffering (Matt. 14:14). He healed Aeneas because He cared for his suffering, and He raised Tabitha from the dead because He cared for the ones she left behind.

God also performs miracles in order to point people to the Savior. Miracles attract attention and open people's hearts to the message of Christ's salvation. We should never use a miracle that God performs to attract attention to ourselves. Rather, we should use it as an opportunity to point people to Jesus. He is the only one who can save them and meet their deepest spiritual needs.

Day 19: Peter Ministers in Judea

Day 20

The Holy Spirit Is Poured Out on the Gentiles

Acts 10:1-48

Have you ever witnessed someone being excluded from a group simply because of their race or tribe? This should never happen among God's people, as Peter learned in today's story.

Caesarea was a great harbor city and the headquarters of the Roman occupation forces. In the city lived a Roman soldier named Cornelius. He was a centurion who commanded one hundred soldiers. Although he was a Gentile, he was a devout, God-fearing man. In spite of this, he still needed to find the way of salvation through Christ.

One day, while he was in prayer, an angel appeared to him in a vision. The angel told him to send messengers to Joppa to fetch a man named Peter who was staying in the home of one Simon the tanner. Cornelius immediately dispatched two of his servants and one devout soldier to go get Peter.

The three men arrived in Joppa at noon on the following day. About that time, Peter went upon the flat roof of Simon's house to

Day 20: The Holy Spirit is Poured Out on the Gentiles

pray. While there, he too was given a vision. In his vision he saw the sky opened and a huge blanket let town from heaven. In the blanket were all kinds of unclean mammals, reptiles, and birds. A voice spoke to Peter ordering him to kill and eat the beasts.

But Peter refused, saying, "No, Lord, I would never eat such unclean food."

The Lord answered him, saying, "Do not call anything impure that God has cleansed." This happened three times, and the blanket was taken back into heaven. Peter wondered, *What is the meaning of this vision?* At that very moment, the three men from Joppa arrived at the house and asked to talk with Peter.

That's when the Holy Spirit said to Peter, "These men have come for you. I sent them, so don't ask questions. Just go with them." The next day Peter went with them back to Caesarea. Six Jewish brothers accompanied him.

When they arrived at Cornelius' home, they found a large group of people gathered for the occasion. Peter addressed them, "As a Jew, all my life I have considered Gentiles to be unclean. But now God has shown me that I was wrong. I should not consider anyone unclean simply because they are of a different race than I." Then he asked, "Why did you send for me?"

Cornelius told Peter about the angel's instructions. "Now," he said, "We are ready to listen to what you have to say."

At that, Peter told them about his vision, and about how God had changed his heart. "Now I know that God opens His arms to people from all tribes and nations," he said. He then told them about Jesus and how God has anointed Him with the Holy Spirit and power, and how He had been crucified and raised from the dead on the third day. Peter continued, "We have been appointed as His witnesses. We are to announce to all that everyone who believes in Christ receives forgiveness of sins through His name" (v. 43).

Then, an amazing thing occurred. While Peter was still speaking, the Holy Spirit came powerfully upon everyone who was listening to his message. And just as the first disciples had done on the Day of Pentecost, they all began to speak in tongues and magnify God. Peter then ordered that they all be baptized in the name of Jesus. "Because," he exulted, "they've received the Holy Spirit exactly as we did!"

The Caesarean Outpouring

This outpouring of the Spirit is another pivotal event in the history of the church. By giving new Gentile believers the Holy Spirit and empowering them as Christ's witnesses, God was opening wide the door of faith to the Gentiles. Not only could Gentiles become part of the community of faith, they could be full participants in God's mission to redeem the nations.

This outpouring of the Spirit is called the Caesarean Outpouring. It is the fifth key outpouring of the Holy Spirit to occur in the Book of Acts. The previous four were as follows:

- Pentecost (2:1-4)
- The Second Jerusalem Outpouring (4:31)
- The Samarian Outpouring (8:15-17)
- The Damascus Outpouring (9:17-18).

Now, God pours out His Spirit a fifth time. Here, the Spirit falls on, fills, and empowers a large group of Gentile converts.

As in the first four key outpourings of the Spirit in Acts, this one results in Spirit-empowered missional witness. The Caesarean Outpouring is yet another fulfillment of Jesus' promise in Acts 1:8:

"But you will receive power when the Holy Spirit comes on you; and you will be my witnesses."

A Divine Appointment

Further, the story of Peter's ministry in Caesarea is another example of a divine appointment in the Book of Acts. In this story, God sovereignly arranged the meeting between Cornelius and Peter. Then, He supernaturally guided each of them into a meeting where Peter could share the word of the Lord with Cornelius and his household.

Because Peter was full of the Holy Spirit, he was able to keep his appointment, and a powerful work was done. Once again, we see the Holy Spirit acting as Superintendent of the Harvest.

From this account, we learn three important missional lessons:

No One is Excluded

The first lesson we learn is that we should exclude no one from the church because of his or her race, tribe, or ethnic background. In a vision, the Holy Spirit taught Peter that he should call no person common or unclean.

We should therefore welcome every person of every race into our church services. Further, we should take deliberate steps to share the gospel with all people. We do this knowing that God has placed in the heart of all people the ability to hear the gospel and be saved.

All Can Participate

A second lesson we learn from the story of Peter's ministry in Caesarea is that everyone who becomes a follower of Christ can also become a full participant in His mission. By filling the new Gentile converts with the Holy Spirit, God was showing Peter and his Jewish

Day 20: The Holy Spirit is Poured Out on the Gentiles

companions that the Gentiles could also take part in God's mission to redeem the lost.

The primary reason Jesus baptizes believers in the Holy Spirit is to empower them as His witnesses. God gave the Holy Spirit to these Gentiles for the same reason He gave the Spirit to the apostles and the other disciples at Pentecost, that is, to enable them to accomplish the work He had given them. That work was to proclaim Christ "in Jerusalem, and in all Judea and Samaria, and to the ends of the earth."

Tongues is a Sign

Finally, from the story of the outpouring of the Spirit on the Gentiles in Caesarea, we learn how speaking in tongues serves as a sign from God that one has been empowered by the Spirit to proclaim the gospel to the lost. This is the second time in Acts that Luke mentions tongues. The first time was on the Day of Pentecost in Acts chapter 2. Now, when the Gentiles in Caesarea are filled with the Spirit, they too speak in tongues and magnify God.

We can magnify the Lord in two ways, by worshipping Him in Spirit and truth and by declaring His greatness to others. As at Pentecost, these newly Spirit-empowered disciples must have magnified God in the same two ways.

Speaking in tongues as the Spirit gives utterance is the initial physical evidence that one has been baptized in the Holy Spirit. It is a sign from God that He has empowered them to speak for Him.

Day 20: The Holy Spirit is Poured Out on the Gentiles

Day 21

A Missionary Church is Born

Acts 11:1-30

The birth of a baby is an exciting event. New life has come into the world. Friends and family are delighted as they search the baby's features for likenesses to the parents. "He has his father's hands!" friends exclaim. Or, "She has her mother's eyes!" As the child grows, it quickly acquires the traits and attitudes of the family.

That's how it is with the birth of a new church. It too is an exciting event. Again, new life comes into the world. And, just as with a human child, the infant church should quickly take on the traits and attitudes of its heavenly family: the Father, Son, and the Holy Spirit. In Acts 11, Luke tells the story of the birth of a new church in the city of Antioch, Syria. As we will learn, the new church quickly takes on the missional nature of its heavenly Father.

Following the Caesarean Outpouring, Peter remained in the city for a few days nurturing the new believers. He then returned to Jerusalem to report to the apostles and elders what had happened in Caesarea. He told them how God himself had opened the door of faith to the Gentiles. Peter explained to them that God "gave the same gift to them as he gave to us" (v. 17). The church leaders in Jerusalem

Day 21: A Missionary Church is Born

were overjoyed when they heard the news, and they rejoiced that God had granted salvation to the Gentiles.

At this point in his story, Luke takes us back several months to the persecution that occurred in Jerusalem. You will remember how Saul raged against the church. In panic, believers fled the city in all directions. Yet amazingly, they "preached the word wherever they went" (6:4).

That's when Philip went to a city in Samaria and proclaimed Christ. Others fled into Phoenicia, Cyprus, and Cyrene on the northern coast of Africa. Luke, however, chooses to focus on the missionary work done by those who travelled to Antioch. He does this because something momentous happened there; a great missionary church was born.

The first wave of refugees to arrive in Antioch began preaching the gospel. However, unlike Philip had done in Samaria, they reached out only to their fellow Jews. This would be natural since they all shared the same heritage, culture, and language. However, it was not what God intended, for the vast majority of those living in Antioch were Gentiles. Antioch was a large multicultural city, and people from many places and cultures intermingled there. While many Jews were coming to the Lord, the large majority of those who lived in Antioch were being overlooked.

Then, a second wave of Jewish Christians arrived in Antioch. These new immigrants came from Cyprus and Cyrene. They did something different from the first wave of Christians to arrive in the city. They not only witnessed to the Jews, they also witnessed to the Greek-speaking Syrians, both Jews and Gentiles. Luke says, "The Lord's hand was with them, and a great number of people believed and turned to the Lord" (v. 21).

Day 21: A Missionary Church is Born

As a result of their Spirit-empowered cross-cultural witness, a strong missionary church formed in Antioch. The church was made up of people from many races.

When the apostles in Jerusalem heard what was happening in Antioch, they sent Barnabas to check it out. Barnabas was a good man, full of the Holy Spirit and faith. When he arrived in Antioch and saw what God was doing, he rejoiced. He then began to encourage the new disciples to wholeheartedly follow Christ. Because of his witness, many people turned to the Lord.

Barnabas then decided to go to Tarsus to fetch Saul. When he found him, he brought him back to Antioch. The two men teamed up and spent a whole year training the Antiochian believers. Large numbers of disciples attended their teaching sessions. For the first time, people began calling them as Christians.

During this time, a prophet named Agabus came from Jerusalem to Antioch. He predicted that a great famine would come to the Roman world. The people agreed that the prophecy was from God. So they received an offering and dispatched Barnabas and Saul to carry it to the needy saints in Jerusalem.

Strategic Location

Antioch, Syria, was an ideal place to establish a great missionary church. It was the third largest city in the Roman Empire, following Rome and Alexandria in Egypt. It was also situated on a major trade route. The church that emerged there was to become Paul's base of missionary operation. From there he would begin each of his three missionary journeys.

Not only was the church strategically located, it had other qualities that make it a great example of what a church should look like. Let's look at seven characteristics of a great missionary church found in the church in Antioch:

Spirit-empowered Ministry

First, we learn that a great missionary church is empowered by the Holy Spirit. Concerning the Antioch church, Luke says that "the Lord's hand was with them" (v. 21). This is another way of saying that the Holy Spirit was powerfully working in their midst. As a result of the Spirit's working through them, "a great number of people believed and turned to the Lord" (v. 21).

Like the Antiochian Christians, we too must ensure that our churches are full of the Holy Spirit and that the Spirit of the Lord is moving powerfully among the people.

Anointed Leadership

Second, we learn that great missionary churches are led by men and women who are full of the Holy Spirit and faith. The Bible says that Barnabas, the leader of the church in Antioch, "was a good man, full of the Holy Spirit and faith, and a great number of people were brought to the Lord" (v. 24). Saul, who joined Barnabas in Antioch, was also full of the Holy Spirit and faith.

If we are to have truly missionary churches, the leadership of the church, beginning with us, must be full of the Holy Spirit and faith.

Outward Focus

A third characteristic of a truly missionary church is outward focus. The church in Antioch aggressively reached out to all the residents of its city. And, as we will learn in upcoming lessons, the church would soon reach out to other nations. It did this by sending

Day 21: A Missionary Church is Born

and supporting Barnabas and Saul as missionaries to various parts of the Roman Empire.

The Christians in Antioch not only reached out to those of their own tribe and race, they reached out to people of all tribes and races. Luke writes, "Some of them…began to speak to Greeks also, telling them the good news about the Lord Jesus" (v. 20). They remembered Jesus' last command and promise in Acts 1:8: "But you will receive power when the Holy Spirit comes on you; and you will be my witnesses in Jerusalem, and in all Judea and Samaria, and to the ends of the earth."

Gospel Proclamation

A fourth characteristic of a great missionary church is that the members faithfully share the message of Christ with others. Luke says that the Antiochian Christians proclaimed "the good news about the Lord Jesus" (v. 20). This is a trait of disciples throughout the Book of Acts. Today, if we would have a great church, we must do the same. We must faithfully share the gospel with everyone.

Missional Training

The fifth characteristic of a great missionary church is that it trains its people in the ways and mission of God. Luke says that Barnabas and Saul "met with the church and taught great numbers of people" (v. 26). They surely taught them the basics of Christian living. They further taught them about God's mission and how they could effectively participate in that mission. We must do the same in our churches today.

Spiritual gifts

A sixth characteristic of a great missionary church is that they allow the gifts of the Spirit to operate in their gatherings, enabling and

Day 21: A Missionary Church is Born

guiding them to do God's will. The prophet Agabus was permitted to speak by the Spirit in the Antioch church and warn of a coming famine. Later in Acts, another prophecy will be given. It will launch Barnabas and Saul into their first missionary journey (13:1-4). We too must cultivate and encourage the manifestation of Spirit gifts in our churches today.

Generosity

Finally, a true missionary church gives generously to advance the work of the kingdom. Once God's will had been revealed to them through the prophecy of Agabus, the disciples in Antioch gave generously to advance the work. Each one gave "according to his ability" (v. 29). Like them, we too must lead the members of our churches into generous missionary giving.

Today, if we would have strong missional churches like the church of Antioch, we must ensure that each of these seven characteristics are present.

Day 22

Persecution, Prayer, and Deliverance

Acts 12:1-25

On my television screen I watched as six men with sabers in hand and black hoods over their heads stood before several kneeling Christians. They were about to execute the Christians by chopping off their heads. The Christians' only "crime" was that they refused to convert to Islam. I prayed for these brave brothers and for their families. In our story today, we learn some lessons on how Christians are to respond when they are being persecuted.

As the great missionary church was emerging in Antioch, back in Jerusalem other momentous events were occurring.

Herod, the Roman king, began lashing out at the church, arresting Christians and throwing them into jail. One day he seized James, the apostle and brother of John, and had him beheaded. Noticing how much this pleased the Jewish authorities, Herod arrested Peter and threw him into prison, intending to do the same with him in a few days.

Day 22: Persecution, Prayer, and Deliverance

When the Christians got wind of this, they began to cry out to God for Peter's deliverance. The day before Peter was to be brought before Herod for sentencing, they met again at the house of Mary, the mother of John Mark, to pray. They prayed into the night.

Meanwhile, Peter lay in his prison cell chained between two guards, sound asleep. Suddenly the chamber was flooded with light. Peter woke up to see a radiant angel standing before him. The angel said to him, "Quick Peter, get up!" At that, the chains fell from Peter's wrists and he arose.

The angel led him past the guards to the main gate of the prison. The gate swung open all by itself, and they walked through it into the street. Then, as suddenly as he had appeared, the angel vanished. Peter was so dazed by all of this that he thought he was seeing a vision. When he finally came to himself, he realized what had happened. The Lord had sent His angel and had delivered him from Herod's clutches. Peter headed for the house where the saints were in prayer for him.

When he arrived, he banged on the outside gate. Hearing the racket outside, a girl named Rhoda went to see what was up. *Wow,* she thought, *it's Peter!* She ran back into the house shouting, "Peter is at the door!" The saints, however, supposed she had lost her wits and refused to believe her. "You are out of your mind," one said. Another surmised, "Maybe she has seen an angel."

In the meantime, Peter was still banging on the gate. When someone did finally open the door, they were all astounded. In their excitement, they were making so much noise that Peter had to quieten them down before he could talk. He then told them how the angel of the Lord had delivered him from prison. After that, he left and went to another place.

The next morning there was a big uproar at the prison when they discovered that Peter was missing. When Herod found out what had happened, he had the guards executed.

Some weeks later, Herod was struck down by the very angel who had led Peter out of the prison. In spite of all of these troubles, the word of God continued to spread and the number of disciples multiplied.

Persecution in Acts

Persecution is a major theme in Acts. From beginning to end, the church advances in the face of hostility. This hostility comes primarily from two sources, from religious leaders and from political authorities. Whenever either group feels threatened, they lash out at Christ's followers.

Luke wrote Acts to show how a church can move forward, even in the face of such persecution. This can happen if Christians will be empowered by the Holy Spirit and remain committed to God's mission. That mission is to reach all people of all nations and tribes with the gospel of Christ. God wants everyone to be a part of His eternal kingdom.

The story of Peter's deliverance from prison teaches us three important lessons on how we can best participate in advancing God's kingdom in the earth, even in the face of persecution and threat.

The Importance of Prayer

First, we learn of the importance of prayer to the work of missions. When the Christians in Jerusalem heard that Peter had been arrested, their first response was to pray. God heard their prayer and delivered Peter from prison.

Someone has said that the army of God best advances on its knees. Of all the weapons in the church's armory, none is more potent than the weapon of prayer.

Throughout the Book of Acts, we read of the saints praying. They prayed in times of great need, as in today's story. They also prayed when seeking for the empowerment of Spirit, when making important decisions, or when seeking God's guidance in mission. We must never be so foolish as to neglect the great weapon of prayer.

Responding to Persecution

Second, in the story of Peter's deliverance from prison, we learn something about how we should respond to persecution. When persecution does come, we should not be surprised. On the contrary, we should be surprised if we are not persecuted. Paul warned Timothy, his son in the faith, "Everyone who wants to live a godly life in Christ Jesus will be persecuted" (2 Tim. 3:12). Peter, who was able to sleep peacefully in prison, later wrote, "Dear friends, do not be surprised at the painful trial you are suffering, as though something strange were happening to you. But rejoice that you participate in the sufferings of Christ" (1 Pet. 4:12-13).

When persecution comes, we should do as Peter and the early Christians did. We should pray, trust in God, and remain full of the Spirit and committed to God's mission.

The Role of Angels

Finally, in the story of Peter's deliverance from prison we learn something about the role of angels in advancing God's kingdom in the earth. This is the fourth time we encounter angels in Acts and the second time an angel delivers Peter from prison.

Day 22: Persecution, Prayer, and Deliverance

In the Book of Acts, angels never appear simply to help individuals achieve their own selfish goals. They always come to direct and assist disciples in pursuing the work of missions. You will remember the first time the angel appeared to Peter in prison. He commanded Peter and John to "Go, stand in the temple courts and tell the people the full message of this new life" (5:20).

Day 22: Persecution, Prayer, and Deliverance

Day 23

The Gentile Mission is Launched

Acts 13:1-4

The wise man said, "There is a time for everything, and a season for every activity under the heavens" (Ecc. 3:1). In the Book of Acts, the time had come for the church to enter into a new era of missions. Up to now missionaries had gone out on their own, or because they were driven out by persecution. Now the time had come for the church to intentionally send out missionaries to unreached peoples and places. God would use the church in Antioch to launch this new era of Gentile missions.

We learned about the church in Antioch a couple of lessons back. There, we saw how the church was founded, and how it developed into a strong, Spirit-empowered missionary church. This was partly because it was blessed with strong spiritual leaders.

Among those leaders were a number of prophets and teachers. Prophets speak by the Spirit encouraging the saints to follow God and pursue His mission. Teachers also speak by the Spirit; however, their main focus is to lead people into a clearer understanding of Scripture. The prophets and teachers in Antioch included Barnabas, whom we have already met in previous lessons; Simeon, who was sometimes called Niger, meaning "the black man"; Lucius from the North African province of Cyrene; and Manaen, who had been brought up with Herod Antipas, the Roman governor.

Saul of Tarsus was also one of the Spirit-anointed ministers in the church in Antioch. He was a prophet, a teacher, and an apostle. Beginning with this story, he becomes the main character for the rest of the Book of Acts.

The church at Antioch entered into a time of prayer and fasting. On one of those days, they gathered for worship. As they waited on the Lord, the Spirit moved powerfully in their midst. One of the prophets lifted up his voice and began to speak. Through him the Holy Spirit said, "Set apart for me Barnabas and Saul for the work to which I have called them" (v. 2). The time had come for the Gentile Mission to commence. It was time for Saul and Barnabas to launch out on their first missionary journey.

This word from the Lord led to more fasting and prayer. Soon, the church elders laid their hands on the two apostles and sent them to the work. Everyone knew, however, that it was not just the church sending them out. They were being sent on their way by the Holy Spirit. Paul and Barnabas set out for the coastal city of Seleucia. From there they sailed for Cyprus, an island in the northeastern Mediterranean Sea.

Launching the Gentile Mission

The move of the Spirit in the church in Antioch marks another milestone in the history of the church. It signals the beginning of the Gentile Mission. Up until now, the church has focused its evangelistic efforts almost entirely on Jews. However, step by step, the Holy Spirit has transformed the church from a local, single-culture mission into an international, multicultural redemptive force. In Acts, Luke traces how the Spirit brought about this transformation.

First, the Spirit of God came upon and filled the mixed-race Samaritans. Next, He transformed and empowered Saul of Tarsus, who was to become the great apostle to the Gentiles. Then, He came upon Cornelius and his household in Caesarea, empowering these new Gentile converts as Christ's witnesses to the lost. In doing this, God was showing that Gentiles could become full participants in God's mission to redeem the nations. The Holy Spirit had opened wide the door for the gospel to go to the ends of the earth.

In similar manner, we should allow the Spirit to move in our local churches today. As we do this, we should explain to the people the missional purpose the Spirit's coming. He will then transform our churches into powerful Spirit-empowered missionary churches just as He did the churches in the Book of Acts.

The Antiochian Outpouring

The Antiochian Outpouring is the sixth key outpouring of the Holy Spirit in the Book of Acts. The previous five were

- Pentecost (2:1-4),
- the Second Jerusalem Outpouring (4:31),
- the Samaritan Outpouring (8:15-17),
- the Damascus Outpouring (9:17-18),
- and the Caesarean Outpouring (10:44-46)

Like these five outpourings, the Antiochian Outpouring is another example of Luke's empowerment-witness motif. You will remember that this pattern was first presented by Jesus in Acts 1:8 when He promised, "You will receive power when the Holy Spirit comes on you and you will be my witnesses."

Now, here in Antioch, another powerful move of the Spirit occurs. This powerful move of the Spirit launches the Gentile Mission. By repeating this pattern over and over throughout the Book of Acts, Luke is emphasizing that every church, and every believer in the church, needs to be empowered by the Spirit to effectively participate in God's mission. Stated another way, any church or believer who will be empowered by—and remain full of—the Holy Spirit can become a powerful witness for Christ.

From the story of the move of the Antioch Outpouring, we learn three more important lessons concerning our participation in God's mission:

The Spirit Calls

First, we learn that the Spirit calls and directs people to participate in God's mission. The Spirit spoke in Antioch, saying, "Set apart for me Barnabas and Saul for the work to which I have called them" (v.2). Once again, the Holy Spirit is acting as the Superintendent of the Harvest. As such, He calls individuals into Christ's service, empowers them as Christ's witnesses, sends them to the work, and then guides them along the way. He will do the same for us today if we will yield our lives completely to Him.

The Church Must Send

A second lesson we learn from this story is that we should strive to develop our churches into strong missions sending bases. The church in Antioch is an example of such a church. At the beginning, the Antiochian Christians only reached out to people from their own tribe and language group. However, as the Spirit continued to move among them, and as they were taught about God and His mission, they were transformed into a missions sending base. This was the church that sent Paul out on each of his three missionary journeys in Acts.

We Must Remain Open

A final lesson we learn from the story of the move of the Spirit in the Antioch church is, if we are to have powerful missionary churches, we must remain open to the moving of the Holy Spirit in our midst. We must ensure that our members have been filled with the Holy Spirit and that they understand their responsibility of actively participating in God's mission.

A truly missionary church, like the church in Antioch, will reach out aggressively in evangelism and church planting. At the same time, it will remain focused on the nations that need to hear the gospel. Such a church will be strong in pastoral care and discipleship training. The gifts of the Spirit will be in operation, and the people will be taught to give generously and sacrificially to the work of missions. The truly missional church will gather often for Spirit-anointed worship and times of intensive prayer and fasting. It is God's will for every local congregation to be a Spirit-empowered missional church.

Day 23: The Gentile Mission is Launched

Day 24

Spirit-Empowered Ministry on Cyprus

Acts 13:5-13

"God told me to do it!" Have you ever been in a situation when someone has made that statement? Then, when they did what they said God wanted them to do, nothing turned out right. So, you wondered, *Did God really speak to them?* Some people do falsely claim that God is speaking to them when He really isn't. However, we should never doubt that God really does speak to His children. In today's story, God speaks to Paul and tells him what He is about to do.

Being sent out by the Holy Spirit, Barnabas and Saul left Syrian Antioch and headed for the coast. They took with them Barnabas' nephew, John Mark. They soon reached the seaport city of Seleucia where they boarded a ship bound for Cyprus. Arriving at Salamis on the southwestern coast of Cyprus, they dropped anchor. As soon as they had disembarked, they went into the Jewish synagogue and proclaimed the word of God.

At this point in our story, an interesting thing occurs. Luke no longer refers to Saul by his Jewish name, "Saul," but begins to call

Day 24: Spirit-Empowered Ministry on Cyprus

him by his Roman name, "Paul." Also, instead of referring to the two missionaries as "Barnabas and Saul," as he has done up to this point, Luke reverses the order and starts referring to them as "Paul and Barnabas."

The two missionaries left Salamis and trekked westward along the island's southern coastline. At every opportunity, they told people about Jesus. Finally, they arrived at Paphos, the capital city of Cyprus. This was the birthplace and home of Barnabas. It was known for its worship of the Greek fertility goddess Aphrodite.

At Paphos the apostles encountered a Jewish sorcerer and false prophet named Bar-Jesus, also known as Elymas. This charlatan had been able to weasel his way into the good graces of Sergius Paulus, the governor of the island. Paulus, however, was an intelligent man and wanted to hear the word of God. So he invited Paul and Barnabas to visit him. Elymas also showed up to challenge the missionaries. He tried to convince the governor to disregard the things Paul was telling him.

But Paul was full of the Holy Spirit, so he was able to hear the voice of the Spirit telling him what God was about to do. So Paul looked at Elymas and declared, "You son of the devil, you enemy of all that is good, you are truly filled with lies and evil. Why do you keep twisting the ways of the Lord? Look! The hand of the Lord is against you. You will be blinded and unable to see the sun for a time."

Immediately a dark mist came over the sorcerer's eyes, and he was unable to see. He began groping around and begging for someone to take him by the hand and lead him. Seeing what the Lord had done, Sergius Paulus immediately believed. He was amazed at the teaching about the Lord.

After this, the three missionaries left Paphos and sailed northward to the port town of Perga located on the southern coast of Pamphylia. They then headed inland until they reached Antioch in Pisidia. John Mark, however, abandoned the work and returned to his home in Jerusalem.

Gifts of the Spirit

In today's story we observe Paul moving in the power of the Holy Spirit. Throughout Acts, Luke presents Paul as a charismatic prophet and apostle. When we say that Paul's ministry was "charismatic," we mean that it was anointed by the Holy Spirit and he often ministered by the gifts of the Spirit. Paul was following in the footsteps of Jesus, who himself carried out His own ministry in the power of the Spirit (Acts 10:38).

The Book of Acts shows us that the gifts of the Holy Spirit are not only intended to operate when God's people have gathered for worship, as Paul presents them in his letters. They are also to be employed by the church when it is scattered in mission. In today's story, God reveals to Paul what He is about to do. This is an example of the gift of discerning of spirits in action.

Power Encounter

Paul's clash with Elymas is a classic example of a power encounter. A power encounter is an open demonstration that the power of God is greater than the power of Satan. It happens when a Spirit-filled disciple directly challenges demonic powers in the name of Jesus.

We must never forget, however, that power ministry is not an end in itself. Our ultimate goal is to bring people to faith in Christ. Therefore, a power encounter (a demonstration of God's power) must always be accompanied by a truth encounter (the proclamation of the gospel). Luke says, "When the proconsul saw what had happened, he believed, for he was amazed at the teaching about the Lord" (v. 12).

From this account of Paul and Barnabas' ministry in the city of Paphos, we learn three more important ministry lessons.

Understand Our Assignment

First, we learn that, like Paul and Barnabas, we must clearly understand our God-given assignments. Paul and Barnabas understood theirs. God had called them to take the gospel to the Gentiles. They also understood what they needed to do to fulfill their calling. They needed to boldly proclaim Christ to the lost and to demonstrate the truth of the message through miraculous signs and wonders.

Today, we have been given the same task. Jesus has command us, "Go into all the world and preach the good news to all creation. Whoever believes and is baptized will be saved, but whoever does not believe will be condemned. And…signs will accompany those who believe…" (Mark 16:15-17).

Be Prepared

Secondly, from Paul and Barnabas' ministry in Paphos, we learn that we must, at all times, be prepared to challenge the forces of evil. Through the Spirit, Paul understood that the devil was working through Elymas the sorcerer. Paul called him a "son of the devil" and "an enemy of all that is good" (v. 10). Later, Paul would write, "We are not unaware of [Satan's] schemes" (2 Cor. 2:11). We can effectively defeat the devil if we will remain full of the Holy Spirit and submissive to the will of God.

Day 24: Spirit-Empowered Ministry on Cyprus

Be Sensitive

Finally, from Paul and Barnabas' ministry in Paphos, we learn that we must be ever sensitive to the Spirit's voice, and we must obey His directives. Luke says that, as Paul was challenging Elymas, he was "filled with the Holy Spirit" (v. 9). This phrase is not describing Paul's initial filling with the Holy Spirit. That happened several years earlier when Ananias laid hands on him in Damascus (9:17-18). This experience of Paul's can more correctly be termed a "refilling" or an "anointing" with the Holy Spirit. Like Peter in Acts 4:8, Paul was being anointed by the Spirit for charismatic ministry.

When we face opposition from Satan, we can be confident that the power of the Spirit is more powerful than that of the enemy. John testified, "The one who is in [us] is greater than the one who is in the world" (1 John 4:4). When involved in ministry, we must trust the Lord to anoint us and to manifest His power through us in the release of spiritual gifts. And, we must trust Him to empower us to boldly proclaim the gospel.

Day 24: Spirit-Empowered Ministry on Cyprus

Day 25

The Gospel is Proclaimed in Pisidian Antioch

Acts 13:13-52

Have you ever been invited to speak to a group of people and then had a difficult time deciding what you were going to talk about? The apostles never struggled with this problem, because they always knew what they were going to say. They were going to tell the people about Jesus and how they could find life by following Him. This fact is demonstrated in our story today, the story of Paul and Barnabas' ministry in Pisidian Antioch.

Leaving Cyprus, the apostles sailed to Perga on the southern coast of Pamphylia. From there they proceeded northward until they arrived at Antioch, a major city of the province of Pisidia. The next Sabbath the two apostles visited a local synagogue. The leader of the synagogue read from the book of the Law then asked Paul if he would like to speak. As was his custom, Paul seized the opportunity to preach the gospel.

Paul began his message by reviewing the many ways God had blessed Israel. The most important way, however, was that He had

Day 25: The Gospel is Proclaimed in Pisidian Antioch

sent to them the message of salvation. "He did this," Paul declared, "by sending Jesus, the descendant of David and Savior of the world."

Tragically, however, the people of Jerusalem and their rulers rejected Jesus and demanded that Pilate execute Him. God, however, vindicated Jesus by raising Him from the dead. "This shouldn't have surprised them," Paul argued, "since it was all foretold by the Hebrew prophets."

Paul continued his message. "Now, through this same Jesus, you can have forgiveness of sins," he said. "Through faith in Him, you can be justified before God, something that the Law of Moses could never do." Paul concluded his message with these strong words: "Therefore, you must not reject Jesus. For, if you do, God will judge you, just as the prophets have warned."

After the meeting, a group gathered around Paul and Barnabas and pleaded with them to come back and tell them more. Many Jews and God-fearing Gentiles followed Paul and Barnabas. The apostles urged them to continue in God's grace.

When the next Sabbath arrived, almost the entire city came out to hear the word of the Lord. This caused some Jews to become jealous. So they began to publically challenge what Paul was saying. The two apostles then turned their attention to the Gentiles.

Quoting the ancient prophet, Paul explained what God had said of him and Barnabas: "I have made you a light for the Gentiles, that you may bring salvation to the ends of the earth" (v. 47; Isa. 49:6; also Acts 1:8). When the Gentiles in the crowd heard them say this, they glorified the Lord.

After these events, the word of the Lord spread through the whole region. The Jews fought back by stirring up some high-ranking city officials, who in turn, whipped up persecution against Paul and

Barnabas. They eventually expelled Paul and Barnabas from the region. The apostles shook the dust from their feet as a sign against them and headed for Iconium. The new disciples they left in Antioch were filled with the Holy Spirit and with joy.

Pisidian Antioch

As we read this story, we must keep in mind that the Antioch spoken of here is different from the Antioch discussed on Days 21 and 23. The previous Antioch was in Syria, this one is in Pisidia, a subdivision of the province of Galatia. The previous Antioch was where Paul and Barnabas began their missionary journey. This Antioch is one of the cities the apostles visited during the journey. It was in this Antioch that Luke narrates Paul's first recorded message in Acts.

Apostolic "Kerygma"

Throughout the book, we will encounter several recorded messages. In fact, in Acts Luke records fifteen sermons spoken by the apostles and other preachers. One was spoken by Stephen, one by James, six by Peter, and seven by Paul. In other places, Luke briefly summarizes the content of the early disciples' messages. For instance, Luke summarizes Philip's ministry in Samaria by saying, "Philip went down to a city in Samaria and proclaimed the Christ there" (8:5).

Luke reports the content of the apostles' preaching for a reason. In Acts 1:8, Jesus told His disciples that they would be His Spirit-empowered witnesses to the ends of their earth. By recording the content of their sermons, Luke is showing his readers what they too should emphasize in their preaching. He is further giving us a clear example of how we should preach today.

Day 25: The Gospel is Proclaimed in Pisidian Antioch

The subject of the apostle's preaching in Acts is sometimes called the "Apostolic Kerygma." (*Kerygma* is the Greek word for proclamation.) As in every other case in Acts, Paul's sermon in Antioch focuses on Jesus. He tells the people who Jesus is, what He has done, and how they should respond to Him.

Jesus is the promised Messiah, the Son of God. He died for our sins on the cross, and he was raised from the dead on the third day. Now, we must all repent of our sins and put our faith in Him alone for salvation. If we will do this, we will be saved. However, if we reject Christ, we will be judged by God.

Some commentators have pointed out how verses 38 and 39 are a summary of the letter that Paul would later write to these same people, known as the book of Galatians. These verses in Acts read, "Therefore, my friends, I want you to know that through Jesus the forgiveness of sins is proclaimed to you. Through Him everyone who believes is justified from everything you could not be justified from by the Law of Moses." (You would do well to memorize these verses.)

In his letter to the Galatians, Paul would write, "A man is not justified by observing the law, but by faith in Jesus Christ. So we, too, have put our faith in Christ Jesus that we may be justified by faith in Christ and not by observing the law, because by observing the law no one will be justified" (2:16).

Faithfully Proclaim Christ

We learn a very important lesson from this story. We learn that, wherever we go we must faithfully proclaim Jesus Christ. We must clearly preach and teach people about Christ's saving work on the cross and His glorious resurrection from the dead. We must tell them that through faith in Him they can receive forgiveness of sins and eternal life. Further, we must let them know that Christ has ascended to the right hand of God. From there He has poured out the Holy Spirit to fill us with His joy and to empower us to reach others with the message of salvation.

Day 25: The Gospel is Proclaimed in Pisidian Antioch

Day 26

Miracles in Iconium, Lystra and Derbe

Acts 14:1-28

The famous German physicist, Albert Einstein, once said, "Nothing truly valuable arises from ambition, or from a mere sense of duty; it stems rather from love and devotion." Today's story from the Book of Acts reveals Paul and Barnabas' love and devotion to God and His mission. We see their love, not so much from their words as from their actions.

Leaving the newly planted church in Pisidian Antioch, the apostles took the route leading southwest until they arrived at Iconium. The next Sabbath they went into the Jewish synagogue and preached the gospel with power and effectiveness, just as they had done in Antioch. Some readily believed, but others fiercely opposed the message. Nevertheless, Paul and Barnabas remained in the city speaking boldly for the Lord. All the while, the Lord confirmed their words with miraculous signs and wonders.

Those who opposed the message organized a gang of Jews and Gentiles who plotted to stone Paul and Barnabas. The apostles got

Day 26: Miracles in Iconium, Lystra and Derbe

wind of the plot and fled to the city of Lystra. There they began preaching.

One day a crowd in Lystra gathered to listen to Paul and Barnabas. In the crowd was a man who had never walked. He had been crippled from birth. As Paul was preaching, his attention was drawn to the man. Perceiving in the Spirit that the man had faith to be healed, Paul ordered him, "Stand up on your feet!" Everyone's mouth fell open as the man sprang to his feet and began to walk around—just as if he'd walked all his life!

The people began to cry out in their local language, "The gods have come down to us in human form!" They called Barnabas "Zeus," and Paul they called "Hermes." The local pagan priest then rounded up some bulls, put wreaths around their necks, and began preparations to sacrifice them to the apostles.

When Paul and Barnabas figured out what was going on, they were horrified. They began tearing their clothes and pleading with the people. "What do you think you are doing?" they asked. "We are only humans like all of you. Besides, the very reason we came here was to tell you to turn from these wretched practices to serve the God who is really alive. He is the one who made heaven and earth and everything else."

The apostles continued, "In the past God may have tolerated such actions, but no more. You can see God's kindness in the way He makes your crops grow in their season. Only He can meet your needs and fills your hearts with joy." After many such words, the people finally abandoned their plan.

About that time, some rabble-rousers arrived from Antioch and Iconium and began poisoning the minds of the people. They whipped

Day 26: Miracles in Iconium, Lystra and Derbe

up an angry mob who dragged Paul outside the city. There they stoned him and left him for dead.

However, some of the new disciples from the city gathered around Paul and prayed. Miraculously, God raised him up! Paul then went back into the city. The following day he and Barnabas left Lystra and traveled to the nearby city of Derbe. Once again, they preached the good news about Christ. The Lord worked with them, and many people turned to God.

Then, doubling back, the apostles retraced their steps through Lystra, Iconium and Antioch. In each city, they spent time strengthening the new disciples. They encouraged them to keep living for Jesus, telling them, "We must pass through many hardships to enter the kingdom of God." After appointing elders in each of the new churches, they prayed and fasted with them. As they departed, they committed them to the Lord in whom they had put their trust.

On their way home, Paul and Barnabas stopped off in Perga where they proclaimed the word of the Lord. Then, sailing from there, they returned to Antioch, Syria, the place where they had begun their missionary journey.

In Antioch, the saints gathered to hear all that God had done through them. They rejoiced when they heard how God has used Paul and Barnabas to open the door of faith to the Gentiles. The two apostles remained in Antioch a long time getting some much needed rest and fellowship with the disciples there.

From this amazing story of Paul and Barnabas' ministry in Iconium, Lystra, and Derbe, we can learn three important lessons about missionary and evangelistic work:

Focus on Proclamation

First, we learn again how important it is that we faithfully proclaim the message of Christ to the lost. This, after all, is the primary task of the church. In Iconium, Paul and Barnabas "spoke so effectively that a great number of Jews and Gentiles believed" (v. 1). In Derbe, "they preached the good news…and won a large number of disciples" (v. 21). And in Lystra, when the people wanted to offer sacrifices to them, Paul declared, "We are bringing you good news telling you to turn from these worthless things to the living God" (v. 15).

We too must focus on proclaiming the gospel to the lost. And we must learn to do it effectively, as Paul and Barnabas did in Iconium. Effectiveness in sharing the good news comes from three sources: a thorough knowledge of Scripture, one's own godly character, and the anointing of the Holy Spirit. We must seek to cultivate all three in our Christian lives and ministries.

Spiritual Gifts in Missions

Second, Paul and Barnabas' ministry in Galatia demonstrates the importance of spiritual gifts in spreading the message of Christ. In Iconium God "confirmed the message of His grace by enabling them to do miraculous signs and wonders" (v. 3). In Lystra, the manifestation of spiritual gifts opened the way for effective evangelism.

By observing closely what happened in Lystra, we can see how, in the apostles' ministries, spiritual gifts often worked together in groups. Paul preached a Spirit-anointed message (a prophetic gift). While doing this, the Spirit enabled him to look into a man's heart and see that he had faith to be healed (a revelation gift). He then acted in the gift of faith and commanded the cripple man to stand on his feet. The man obeyed, and a miracle occurred (a power gift). As a result of this tandem manifestation of spiritual gifts, the people believed and turned to Christ.

To be truly effective witnesses and ministers of the gospel, we too must know how to hear the voice of the Spirit. As we respond to His promptings, He will use us to minister spiritual gifts. We must never forget that Christian ministry involves more than just talking. It involves hearing and obeying the voice of the Spirit. It also involves preaching and teaching the gospel under an anointing of the Spirit.

Finally, it involves acting in faith and allowing the Spirit to minister through us through prophetic words and miracles of healing and deliverance. If this is to happen in our lives and ministries, we, like Paul and Barnabas, must learn to minister in the power of the Holy Spirit.

Devotion to the Work

Third, from the story of the apostles' ministry in Iconium, Lystra, and Derbe, we learn the importance of devotion to the Lord and to His mission. Such devotion prompted Paul and Barnabas to go to the field. That same devotion kept them there.

In Iconium, the Jews and Gentiles plotted to stone them, yet the Bible says, "They spent considerable time there, speaking boldly for the Lord" (v. 3). When they were eventually forced to leave the city, they went to "Lystra and Derbe and to the surrounding country, where they continued to preach the good news" (vv. 6-7). Paul was stoned in Lystra, dragged out of the city, and left to die. Yet he went back into the city and continued to preach the gospel.

We cannot let opposition keep us from preaching Christ to all who will listen. When we go out to preach the gospel, we cannot expect everyone to receive our message. Some, however, will.

Day 26: Miracles in Iconium, Lystra and Derbe

Whatever the case, we must continue to preach the good news as long as God wants us to remain in an area. Such boldness comes only as we remain full of the Holy Spirit and fully devoted to Christ and His work.

Day 27

Missionary Council in Jerusalem

Acts 15:1-34

Have you ever attended a church business meeting? You know, one of those meetings where the members get together to discuss the "business matters" of the church. How would you describe the meeting? Was it boring? Quarrelsome? Petty?

Have you ever thought seriously about such meetings? What should be discussed, and what principles should guide the discussion? In today's story from the Book of Acts, the church gathered for a business meeting. And it was one of the most momentous happenings in the history of the Early Church.

Following their first missionary journey, Paul and Barnabas returned to their home city of Antioch. While they were there, some Jewish brothers arrived from Judea. They started teaching that, before a Gentile man could become a Christian, he must first be circumcised according to the Law of Moses. This notion so disturbed Paul and Barnabas that a heated argument broke out.

So the church leaders appointed Paul and Barnabas to lead a delegation to go to Jerusalem. They were to discuss the issue with the apostles and elders there.

Day 27: Missionary Council in Jerusalem

When the delegation arrived in Jerusalem, a special meeting was arranged to discuss the issue. During the meeting, Peter stood up and addressed the delegates. He reminded them of how the Spirit of God had led him to Caesarea to preach the gospel to the Gentiles in Cornelius' home. He then recounted how God had poured out the Holy Spirit on the Gentiles. It was just as He had done on the Jewish believers on the Day of Pentecost.

Peter concluded his speech by emphasizing how God had purified the Gentiles hearts by faith. He then drove his point home, asking, "Now then, why do you try to test God by putting on the necks of the disciples a yoke that neither we nor our fathers have been able to bear? No! We believe it is through the grace of our Lord Jesus that we are saved, just as they are" (vv. 10-11).

Then, everyone listened in hushed silence as Paul and Barnabas told of how God had performed many wonderful miracles among the Gentiles through them.

Finally, James stood to his feet. "Brothers," he said, "listen to me. The stories that Peter and Paul have shared with us go right along with what the prophets said would happen. You remember how, through the prophet Amos, God promised, 'After this I will return and rebuild David's fallen tent... I will restore it, that the remnant of men may seek the Lord, and all the Gentiles who bear my name" (vv. 16-17).

Speaking by the Spirit, James continued, "So, here is my judgment on the matter. We would do wrong to make it hard for the Gentiles to turn to God. Instead, we should write them a letter and tell them what we have decided." Everyone agreed with James' proposal. So they chose some delegates to accompany Paul and Barnabas and carry a letter back to the church in Antioch.

Day 27: Missionary Council in Jerusalem

In the letter, the leaders of the church assured the saints in Antioch that the troublesome men from Judea had not been sent by them. They concluded the letter by saying, "It seemed good to the Holy Spirit and to us not to burden you with anything beyond the following requirements: You are to abstain from food sacrificed to idols, from blood, from the meat of strangled animals and from sexual immorality. Farewell" (vv. 28-29).

When the letter was read to the church in Antioch, everyone rejoiced. All were encouraged by what it said. They knew that a wide door had been opened for them to offer to the Gentiles God's free gift of salvation through faith.

James the Just

As we think about this story, we should keep in mind that the James spoken of here is not James the apostle and brother of John, the one whom Herod killed. The James spoken of here is James, the half-brother of Jesus and pastor of the Jerusalem church. He is sometimes referred to as James the Just.

This story of the missionary council in Jerusalem teaches three important lessons concerning how we may best conduct the business of the church today:

Focus on the Mission

The first lesson we learn is that our church business meetings should deal with important matters. In the Jerusalem Council, the delegates did not discuss trivial issues, such as how to decorate the church building or the color of the curtains. They discussed weighty matters affecting the eternal destiny of millions of Gentiles. They were seeking to discover the best way to reach the Gentile nations for Christ.

While less weighty matters must certainly be discussed in our church business meetings, we must never allow them to dominate our discussion. Rather, we must remain focused on real business of the kingdom, reaching the lost for Christ. Jesus said that we were to be His witnesses "in Jerusalem, and in all Judea and Samaria, and to the ends of the earth" (Acts 1:8).

Every discussion, no matter how large or small, must be guided by the question, "How will our decision affect the church's ability to advance the kingdom of God at home and to the ends of the earth?"

Follow Scripture

A second lesson we learn from today's story is that, in conducting the business of the church, all of our decisions must be based squarely upon the teachings of Scripture. When, James announced the decision of the council, he cited Amos 9:11-12. In that text the prophet told of a day when God would take out "from the Gentiles a people for himself" (v. 14).

In other words, their decision was based upon the word of God. James was saying, through Jesus the Son of David the way had been made for Gentiles to seek the Lord.

Today, we must do the same. Every decision we make must be based on the teachings of the Bible. Any decision that will lead us away from God's plan as revealed in God's word must be rejected.

Listen to the Spirit

We can learn a third lesson from the story of the missionary council in Jerusalem. In conducting the business of the church, we must be attentive to the voice of the Spirit. In their letter to the Gentile believers in Antioch, the leaders said that their decision "seemed good to the Holy Spirit." This means that their discussions

Day 27: Missionary Council in Jerusalem

and final decision were guided by the Holy Spirit. As a result, great joy came to the congregation. More importantly, a pathway was created that enabled the church to continue to expand among the Gentiles.

Today, we must do the same. In conducting the business of the church, we must remain focused on the mission of reaching the lost with the gospel, and every decision we make must be based on Scripture. Further, in all that we do, we must listen to and obey the voice of the Holy Spirit. If we will do these things, great blessing will come to the church, and the work of missions will be advanced.

Day 27: Missionary Council in Jerusalem

Day 28

Paul's Second Journey Begins

Acts 15:35-40

In the work of missions, what is more important, the work or the worker? This is an important question, and it is not so easy to answer. Today's story from the Book of Acts teaches us that both the work and the worker are important.

Paul and Barnabas delivered the important letter from the Jerusalem Council to the saints in Antioch. They then began to fervently preach and teach the word of the Lord there. This went on for quite a while. That's when the Spirit of the Lord began to stir Paul's heart.

One day he approached Barnabas and said, "Now is the time for us to revisit all the places where we preached the word of the Lord. We should check and see how the disciples in those places are doing."

Barnabas wanted to take his young cousin John Mark with them. You will remember how John Mark had gone with the two apostles on their first missionary journey. However, partway through the mission, he had abandoned the work and returned home. Because of this, Paul did not want to take Mark with them.

Day 28: Paul's Second Journey Begins

A big argument broke out between the two missionaries, with neither one willing to back down. Their dispute became so heated that they finally agreed to go their separate ways. Barnabas would revisit Cyprus and Paul would go to southern Galatia.

So Barnabas took Mark and sailed for Cyprus.

Paul chose Silas as his new associate. The brothers in Antioch then entrusted them into the Lord's care and sent them on their way. Paul and Silas headed through northern Syria and then westward into Cilicia. Everywhere they went, they took time to strengthen the churches.

Paul's Pastoral Heart

From the New Testament we learn that the focus of Paul's ministry was reaching the unreached Gentile nations for Christ. He once testified, "It has always been my ambition to preach the gospel where Christ was not known" (Rom. 15:20). Because of this, he was always going to new places to preach the good news about Christ.

We must not think, however, that Paul's concern for the churches ended once he had established them and moved on to new locations. He wrote the believers in Corinth telling them of his "deep concern for all of the churches" (2 Cor. 11:28). Whenever he had opportunity, Paul always returned to these churches to strengthen and encourage the disciples there.

This is what happened in today's story. Paul said to Barnabas, "Let us go back and visit the brothers in all the towns where we preached the word of the Lord and see how they are doing" (v. 36).

Paul's motive for revisiting the churches was to strengthen the brothers and sisters in those places. For this same reason, he wrote letters to the churches. Paul wanted every church he planted to

Day 28: Paul's Second Journey Begins

emerge as a Spirit-empowered missionary church—one that could extend itself into the surrounding region. We today must have the same goal for our churches.

From the story of the controversy between Paul and Barnabas, we learn three more valuable lessons concerning the work of the Lord. The first lesson we learn from Barnabas, the second we learn from Paul, and the third we learn from both apostles.

Trust People in Ministry

From the actions of Barnabas, we learn the value of trusting people and giving them a second chance in ministry. During Paul and Barnabas' first missionary journey, Mark had forsaken the work and returned home. Because of this, Paul did not want him to join them on their second journey. Barnabas, however, saw potential in his young cousin. He wanted to give him a second chance, so he took Mark with him to revisit Cyprus.

Barnabas was right in giving Mark a second chance. For ultimately the young man did well. We know this because, years later, Paul referred to Mark as his "fellow worker" in the Lord's work (Phil. 1:24). When Paul was in a Roman prison, he wrote Timothy and asked him to "get Mark and bring him with you, because he is helpful to me in my ministry" (2 Tim. 4:11). Mark would eventually go on to write the gospel that bears his name.

So, from Barnabas we learn the importance of trusting people and giving them a second chance in ministry.

The Importance of the Mission

We also learn a valuable lesson from the actions of Paul on this occasion. From him, we learn of the importance of fulfilling our God-given mission. While Barnabas was concerned about Mark, Paul was

Day 28: Paul's Second Journey Begins

focused on accomplishing the mission. Christ had commissioned him to plant the church among the Gentiles. Paul was so devoted to fulfilling this mission that he refused to allow anything to hinder its accomplishment. During the first journey, Mark had proven to be an unreliable partner. Now, Paul was afraid that his presence on the team would hinder the work.

Paul was right in guarding the mission. For reaching the lost is the church's most important duty. Possibly Mark could never have endured the great hardships that Paul and Silas were to face. During this long arduous journey into Asia Minor and pagan Europe, their lives were in constant danger. They traveled great distances over bandit-infested roads. They were mocked, beaten, imprisoned, and driven out of cities. However, to Paul, none of these things mattered. What mattered to him was accomplishing the work that Christ had given him. He would allow nothing to deter him.

From Paul we learn that reaching the lost is so important we should not allow anything to hinder us from fulfilling our mission.

Stay with the Work

We learn a third important lesson from the actions of both Paul and Barnabas on that day. We learn that whatever happens, we must stay with the work. After their heated debate over John Mark, Paul and Barnabas went their separate ways. Barnabas sailed for Cyprus with John Mark, and Paul headed for Asia Minor with Silas.

What is important, however, is that neither man abandoned the work. Both continued as active missionaries. Rather than allow their misunderstanding to stop the work, they entered into a strategic agreement concerning who would go where. Thus, the work was expanded; one effective missionary team became two.

Day 28: Paul's Second Journey Begins

At times Christian brothers and sisters will disagree. When this happens, we should not be tempted to abandon the work God has given us. Like Paul and Barnabas, we must be mature enough to come to strategic agreements on how each will continue in the work. If we remain kindhearted and mature in our attitudes, then in time, even greater unity and agreement can come.

Day 28: Paul's Second Journey Begins

Day 29

The Spirit Guides the Missionaries

Acts 16:1-10

Jesus has commanded us to take the gospel to the whole world. But the world is immense. So many people in so many places need to hear about Christ. To which place should we go first? Paul and Silas faced that same dilemma during Paul's second missionary journey. However, the Spirit of God directed them to where He wanted them to go. He'll do the same for us today.

Leaving their home base of Antioch, Paul and Silas traveled northward through Syria. They then turned westward into Cilicia, Paul's home country. From there they again headed north through the Cilician Gates into southern Galatia. Everywhere they found a local church, they spent time teaching and encouraging the disciples there.

In Lystra they met a young disciple named Timothy. His mother was a Jewish believer, and his father was Greek. Everyone in the region had good things to say about him. Paul also noticed Timothy's high character and strong commitment to Christ, so he asked him to join their missionary team. When Paul discovered that his mixed race

Day 29: The Spirit Guides the Missionaries

troubled some of the local Jews, he arranged for Timothy to be circumcised.

The apostles then moved from town to town teaching believers and sharing the instructions contained in the letter from the Jerusalem Council. The churches were strengthened and continued to grow in numbers daily.

After this, Paul and his missionary team decided to proceed westward into Asia Minor. The Holy Spirit, however, prevented them from going there. So they headed out in a northwesterly direction through Phrygia and Galatia. Coming to the border of Mysia, they decided to head due north into the province of Bithynia. Again, the "Spirit of Jesus" prevented them, and again they adjusted their course. They journeyed to Troas, a seaport on the banks of the Aegean Sea.

During the night Paul was given a vision. In the vision he saw a man from Macedonia standing and pleading with him. The man begged Paul, "Come over to Macedonia and help us" (v. 9). When Paul shared his vision with his colleagues, they concluded that God was directing them to go to Macedonia and declare the message of Christ. They immediately obeyed and sailed for Macedonia.

The Spirit of Jesus

In Scripture, the Holy Spirit is called by many names. For example, He is referred to as the Spirit of God, the Spirit of Truth, and the Counselor. Each name tells us something about His character and work.

In today's story, the Holy Spirit is called "the Spirit of Jesus" (v. 7). This is because He was acting in Jesus' place. He was guiding the missionaries to do the work their Lord had commissioned them to do. In their letters. Paul calls the Holy Spirit "the Spirit of Jesus

Christ" (Phil. 1:19) and Peter refers to Him as "the Spirit of Christ" (1 Pet. 1:11).

Luke Joins the Team

Another interesting thing happens in this passage. When referring to Paul and his missionary band, Luke begins to use the word "we" in place of the word "they," which he has been using up to this point. This tells us that in Troas Luke joined Paul's missionary team. The team now consists of Paul, Silas, Timothy, and Luke.

Luke will accompany Paul as far as Philippi, where he will remain behind. Later in Acts, Paul will find Luke again in Troas. There Luke will rejoin Paul and stay with him through the remainder of the book. This knowledge gives us great confidence in what Luke tells us in the Book of Acts. We know that he was an eyewitness to many of its events.

From the story of how the Spirit directed Paul and his team to Macedonia, we learn two important ministry lessons:

The Value of Ministry Teams

First, we learn the value of ministering in teams. Paul seldom traveled alone. He almost always took people with him to do ministry. He did this for at least two reasons. First, his companions could help him fulfill the calling God had placed on his life. Second, he was able to mentor them in how to be effective missionaries.

One important job of any Christian pastor or leader is to build a good team. These people will help him or her to do their job more efficiently. They will be able to mentor them in the work of the Lord.

However, Paul was very careful about whom he invited to join his team. He always chose people of high character, deep spirituality, and strong commitment to the work of missions. We see this in his choosing Silas, Timothy, and Luke to join him in the mission. No doubt he, like Jesus, also sought the Spirit's guidance in making his choices. We, too, must choose our team members wisely.

The Necessity of Divine Guidance

The second lesson we learn from today's story is the necessity of divine guidance in evangelistic and missionary work. In the story, we again see the Holy Spirit acting as Superintendent of the Harvest. Throughout Acts, He is the one who directs the mission, telling the missionaries where to go and what to do. We have previously seen Him directing Philip into Gaza to talk to the Ethiopian nobleman. He also sent Peter to Caesarea to preach to the household of Cornelius.

Now, in today's story, Luke gives us a detailed account of how the Spirit directed Paul and his team to go into Europe to proclaim the gospel. Once the missionaries determined that the vision was from God, they immediately obeyed and sailed for Macedonia.

In like manner, when we are doing the Lord's work, we should trust the Holy Spirit to guide us. This guidance may come in various ways, including dreams, visions, angelic appearances, and providential circumstances. However, the most usual way God leads us is by speaking directly to our spirits by His Spirit.

To experience such guidance it is essential that we be prayerful and remain full of the Holy Spirit. We should also know that what the Lord speaks to us by the His Spirit will always be in harmony with His written word, the Bible. Then, when the Spirit speaks, we must be quick to obey His voice.

Day 30

The Gospel Goes to Europe

Acts 16:11-15

I once served on a church planning committee. The members of the committee were full of ideas and often put together great plans. The problem was that no one ever got around to carrying out the plans. As a result, little was accomplished. In time, I became frustrated with the committee and moved on to other more productive pursuits.

Paul and his missionary team were not like this committee. Once they had determined that Paul's vision of the man from Macedonia was from God, they immediately moved into action. They boarded a ship and sailed for Macedonia. Landing in Neopolis, they proceeded to the city of Philippi.

The next Sabbath the missionaries went to the nearby river in search of a good place to pray. Upon arriving, they encountered a group of Jewish women. After greeting them, they sat down and began to talk. One of them was a businesswoman from Thyatira named Lydia. She was a seller of expensive purple cloth. She was also a worshipper of God. As Lydia listened to Paul talk about Jesus, the Lord opened her heart and she believed the good news.

Soon she and other members of her household were baptized in water. That's when she approached the missionaries and said, "If you consider me a believer in the Lord, come and stay at my house." At first, the apostles were reluctant to impose upon her, but because she insisted, they took her up on her offer.

The Church at Philippi

Philippi was a chief city of the Roman province of Macedonia, and it was the first place Paul preached in Europe. While there, Paul planted what was to become a thriving church. Paul would later write a letter to the Philippians to encourage the brothers and sisters there.

In this letter, Paul called the Philippian believers his "dear friends." He referred to them as his brothers and sisters whom he loved and longed for (Phil. 4:1). Paul truly loved the people he ministered to. We should do the same; we should love those whom God has given into our care.

The Spirit's Work in Nonbelievers

In the story of Lydia's conversion we see the Spirit of God working in the heart of a Gentile nonbeliever. Luke tells us that, even before she was saved, "the Lord opened her heart to respond to Paul's message" (v. 14). Earlier in Acts, the Spirit worked in the heart of Cornelius before he came to Christ. The Holy Spirit gave him a vision of the Lord who told him to send for Peter. When Peter arrived, he told Cornelius how to be saved.

In each of these stories, we observe how the Spirit of God works in the hearts of nonbelievers. The Spirit draws them to God and opens their hearts to receive the gospel. Further, when sinners repent of their sins and put their faith in Christ for salvation, the Holy Spirit regenerates them, making them new creations in Christ (John 3:7; 2 Cor. 5:17). This is what happened to Lydia and Cornelius.

Women in Ministry

From the story of Lydia's conversion, we learn another important ministry lesson. Here, as he often does in the Book of Acts, Luke emphasizes the role of committed women in advancing the kingdom of God.

For instance, he begins Acts by telling how women gathered with men to pray and wait for the outpouring of the Spirit at Pentecost (1:14). Jesus gave the women the same command He gave to the men. They were to "stay in the city until [they had been] clothed with power from on high" (Luke 24:49).

Then, when the Holy Spirit was poured out at Pentecost, the women were filled with the Spirit, just as the men were. Luke says, *"All of them* were filled with the Holy Spirit and began to speak in other tongues as the Spirit enabled them" (2:4). The Spirit thus empowered the women for the same reason He empowered the men, that they might "be [Christ's] witnesses in Jerusalem, and in all Judea and Samaria, and to the ends of the earth" (1:8).

Then, when Peter stood to explain what had happened, he quoted from the prophecy of Joel where God promised, "In the last days…I will pour out my Spirit on all people. Your sons *and daughters* will prophesy" (2:17). Thus, women are qualified for ministry in the same way that men are qualified, the Lord empowers them by His Holy Spirit.

Now, in today's story, Luke emphasizes that Lydia was the first convert in Europe. A woman thus played a major role in the founding of the church in Philippi. Later in Acts, Luke will tell how a woman named Priscilla, along with her husband Aquila, served with Paul as "fellow workers in Christ Jesus" (Rom. 16:3). She led the way in instructing the mighty preacher, Apollos, and helping him to understand the ways of God more clearly (Acts 18:26). Luke further writes of Philip's four unmarried daughters who served God as prophets (21:9).

More recently, Spirit-filled women have played a key role in the global advance of the modern Pentecostal movement. They have served the church as pastors, missionaries, writers, teachers, and in many other vital ways.

We should thank God for the women who have committed themselves to the work of God. And we should support them and encourage them in their ministries.

Day 31

Imprisonment and Deliverance in Philippi

Acts 16:16-40

During their time in Philippi, Paul and his missionary team stayed with Lydia in her home. One day as they were on their way to a prayer meeting, they met a slave girl who was possessed by an evil spirit. She began to follow them around, and day after day kept shouting, "These men are servants of the Most High God. They will tell you how to be saved."

Finally, Paul became so annoyed that he turned to the girl and spoke directly to the demon inside her. "In the name of Jesus Christ," he commanded, "come out of her!" Immediately, the demon left her. She was free!

This did not sit well with her owners because they were using her demonic ability to predict the future to earn money for themselves. So they seized Paul and Silas and dragged them into the marketplace. There, they set them before the local authorities. "These Jews have the whole city in an uproar," they complained, "They are even teaching people to break the law."

Day 31: Imprisonment Deliverance in Philippi

Hearing what was going on, a mob began to form. So without even looking into the facts of the matter, the magistrates ordered the two missionaries to be stripped and beaten with rods. They then flogged them and threw them into prison. To ensure that they did not escape, the jailer put them into the inner dungeon and clamped their feet in stocks.

Around midnight Paul and Silas began to pray and sing hymns to the Lord. The other prisoners listened as they sang. Suddenly, the place began to quake violently. This caused the cell doors to fly open. Miraculously the chains began to fall from the prisoners' feet. The jailer woke up and noticed the doors standing wide open. Assuming the prisoners had escaped, he drew his knife and was about to commit suicide. When Paul saw this, he shouted at him, "Stop! Don't kill yourself! We are all here!"

Hearing this, the jailer ran up to Paul and Silas and fell down before them trembling. "Sirs," he pleaded, "what must I do to be saved?"

Paul answered, "Believe in the Lord Jesus, and you will be saved—you and your household" (v. 31). He then they took time to teach the jailer and his family about the Lord. The jailer in turn ministered unto the missionaries by washing their wounds and serving them a meal. Paul and Silas then baptized the man and his family in water. Everyone's heart was filled with joy because they had found the Lord.

The next morning the city officials sent the police to Paul and Silas. "You are free to leave in peace," they told them.

But Paul would have none of this. "We are Roman citizens," he said. "You had no right to beat us, but you did anyway. Then you put us in prison. Now you expect us to sneak of out of town. I don't think so. Let the city officials come and publicly escort us out of town."

Day 31: Imprisonment Deliverance in Philippi

The police reported this back to the city officials. They were alarmed to find out that Paul and Silas were Roman citizens. So they went back to the jail and apologized to them for what they had done. They then urged the Paul and Silas to leave the city at once. The apostles, however, went to Lydia's home where they met with the brothers and sisters and encouraged them in the Lord. Then, judging that their work in Philippi was done, they set out for Thessalonica.

From the story of Paul and Silas' missionary work in Philippi, we learn three important ministry lessons:

Spirit-empowered Ministry

First, the account of the deliverance of the slave girl again reminds us of how important it is that we, as Christ's witnesses, be able to minister in the power of the Holy Spirit. Through the spiritual gift of discerning of spirits, Paul determined that the girl was possessed by a demon. Then, through the gift of miraculous powers, he drove the spirit out of her.

In the same way, every minister of Christ should be filled with the Spirit, and they must know how to operate in the gifts of the Holy Spirit. Had Paul not been able to do this, the slave girl would have remained in bondage. Further, his and Silas' ministry in Philippi would have been much less effective.

The Bible commands us to "be filled with the Spirit" (Eph. 5:18). It further commands us to "eagerly desire spiritual gifts" (1 Cor. 14:1). Those who ignore these commands can never be the effective ministers of the gospel that God intends for them to be.

The Joy of the Lord

Secondly, from the story of Paul and Silas' deliverance from jail, we learn how the Spirit can give us joy in times of trial. Such joy can be a powerful witness to others. Paul and Silas prayed and sang

Day 31: Imprisonment Deliverance in Philippi

hymns of joy while in the worst part of the prison. As they sang, the other prisoners listened. Their Spirit-prompted worship was a powerful witness to the other prisoners. It helped to open their hearts to the message of the gospel.

Joy during times of trial is an evidence that one is full of the Spirit. As we abide in Christ, walk in the Spirit, and obey the Lord's commands, our lives will be filled with the joy of the Lord. Such joyful lives will serve as a witness to those who observe us. As a result, they too will be encouraged to follow Christ.

Believe on Jesus

Finally, from today's story, we learn how to be better witnesses for Christ. When the Philippian jailer inquired about how to be saved, Paul and Silas were ready with an answer. They told him, "Believe on the Lord Jesus Christ and you will be saved." The Bible teaches that the two essential elements of true saving faith are repentance toward God and faith toward the Lord Jesus (Acts 20:21).

Repentance toward God involves acknowledging one's sins, asking forgiveness, and turning from sin to walk in newness of life. Faith toward the Lord Jesus involves believing in His death and resurrection, inviting Him into one's life as Lord and Savior, and trusting Him alone for salvation.

Every Christian should, at all times, be prepared to answer the question, "What must I do to be saved?" It is the responsibility of pastors and other church leaders to train everyone in the church how to lead others to Christ.

Day 32

Ministry in Thessalonica and Berea

Acts 17:1-15

In my years as a pastor and missionary I have had people oppose what I was trying to accomplish in ministry. However, I have never experienced the kind of opposition that Paul and his colleagues encountered during their time in Thessalonica and Berea.

Leaving Philippi, Paul and his missionary team travelled westward to Thessalonica, the capital city of Macedonia. For the next three Sabbaths, Paul went to the local Jewish synagogue and discussed the Scriptures with them. He showed them how the Messiah had to suffer and rise from the dead. Paul kept telling them, "This Jesus I am proclaiming to you is the Christ" (v. 3).

Some of the Jews believed, along with a large number of God fearing Greeks, both men women. This caused some prominent Jews to become jealous. So they went to the marketplace, rounded up some local thugs, and formed a mob. Together they incited a riot.

Then some of them went to Jason's house where they heard the apostles were staying. They wanted to seize Paul and Silas and publicly humiliate them. However, when they did not find the apostles there, they grabbed Jason and some other brothers and dragged them out. They then shouted to the crowd, "These men have caused trouble all over the world. Now, here they are in our city doing the same thing. And this Jason fellow has welcomed them into his home. They profess allegiance to a king other than Caesar, a man by the name of Jesus. This is nothing less than treason!"

When the people of the city heard this, mayhem broke out. Everyone, including the city officials, was thrown into a state of frenzy. Eventually, after things had died down, they allowed Jason and the brothers to post bond and let them go. When darkness came, some of the new Christian brothers led Paul and Silas to the edge of the city and sent them on their way to Berea.

When the apostles arrived in Berea, they went to the synagogue. They happily discovered that the Bereans were nobler than the citizens of Thessalonica, for they eagerly received the good news about Jesus. Every day the Bereans gathered to examine the Scriptures to see if Paul's words were true. Because of this, many Jews believed, along with several leading women.

When word of what was happening in Berea got back to the Jews of Thessalonica, they sent some ruffians to Berea. These men began whipping up the crowds there, just as they had done in Thessalonica. Because Paul was their primary target, the brothers whisked him off to the coast and put him on a ship headed for Athens. Silas and Timothy, however, stayed at Berea to encourage the believers.

From this story, we can learn three powerful ministry lessons:

Systematic Bible Study

First, we learn about how important it is for us to systematically teach the Scriptures to the people. Paul's ministry in Macedonia was marked by such a thorough and organized approach to teaching. The

Bible tells us that in Thessalonica he went repeatedly into the synagogue where he "reasoned with them from the Scriptures, explaining and proving that the Christ had to suffer and rise from the dead" (17:2-3). Then, when he arrived in Berea, Paul met with the people there "and examined the Scriptures every day" (v. 11).

Like Paul, we too should commit ourselves to systematically teaching Scripture in our churches. As we do, we should keep one fact in mind; Jesus is the central message and true fulfillment of all Scripture, both Old and New Testaments.

Anointed Teaching

Secondly, from the story of Paul's missionary work in Thessalonica and Berea, we learn that our teaching, just like our preaching, should be anointed by the Holy Spirit. Paul wrote a follow-up letter to the Christians in Thessalonica. In it, he reminded them how he had taught them the word of God "with power, with the Holy Spirit and with deep conviction" (1 Thess. 1:5). He further reminded them how they had "welcomed the message with the joy given by the Holy Spirit." As a result of this Spirit-anointed teaching, the church in Thessalonica became "a model to all the believers in Macedonia and Achaia." Then, from there "the Lord's message rang out" to the surrounding regions (vv. 6-8).

The same is true today. If we want powerful, Spirit-anointed churches, we must systematically teach God's Word with the anointing of the Holy Spirit.

The Gospel Will Prevail

The third lesson we learn from this story is that we can expect the truth of the gospel to prevail even in the face of strong opposition. In both Thessalonica and Berea, certain elements of the population

Day 32: Ministry in Thessalonica and Berea

opposed Paul's ministry. However, in both places, people accepted the Lord and strong churches were planted.

We can expect the same thing to occur when we go to new places to preach the gospel and plant churches. Paul once wrote, "I am not ashamed of the gospel, because it is the power of God that brings salvation to everyone who believes" (Rom. 1:16).

We can have the same faith in the gospel message. While some will oppose it, we must faithfully preach and teach the good news about Jesus and remain full of the Holy Spirit. If we will do this, some will receive the message with joy and strong churches will be planted.

Day 33

Paul Preaches in Athens

Acts 17:16-34

Do you live in a place where people of different cultures and backgrounds reside? If so, have you tried to reach out to someone of a different culture than your own? God expects us to share Christ with all people. However, to effectively do that we must know how to adapt our approach to the culture we are trying to reach. In today's lesson, we discover how Paul did this very thing. He adapted his preaching to reach out to two very different cultures.

Leaving Berea, Paul journeyed to Athens, the capital city of Greece and the cultural center of the Roman Empire. There, he observed the city's magnificent temples and celebrated works of art. However, rather than being impressed with their great beauty, he was distressed by the pagan worship they represented.

As was his custom, each Sabbath day Paul went to the synagogue to discuss the Scriptures with the Jews and God-fearing Greeks. On other days, he went into the marketplace, known as the Agora, and reasoned with the Greek scholars there.

One day, a group of philosophers began a conversation with Paul. He used the opportunity to tell them how Jesus had died for their sins

Day 33: Paul Preaches in Athens

and rose on the third day. When they heard this, they began to mock him. "This babbler seems to be advocating some foreign gods," they said. "Does he really expect us to believe his wild story?" They then took him to Mars Hill, the place where the chief magistrates of the city met. There they interrogated him, "You have been teaching some strange ideas in the city. Tell us what you mean by these things."

Paul had been looking for this opening. So he rose to his feet and addressed the assembly. "Men of Athens," be began, "I notice that you are a very religious people. As I was walking around your city, I saw many monuments to your gods. One in particular had this inscription on it: 'To an Unknown God.'

" I have come to tell you who that God is! He is the one who created the world and everything in it. Being the Lord of all heaven and earth, He does not live in man-made temples like the ones we see here. He needs no human to take care of Him, for He is the one who gives life and breath to every living thing."

Paul turned, and motioning with his hand, he continued, "From one man, God made every nation in the whole earth, and He sovereignly decides where they should live and when and how they should rise and fall. He does this so that people will seek Him, and hopefully find Him.

"However, in truth, He is not far from any one of us. For in Him we live and move and have our being. Even your own poets have declared, 'We are God's offspring.' Therefore, since we have all been created by God, we should not think of Him as being some humanly carved idol, no matter how skillfully it may have been fashioned."

Paul then began to drive his message home. "There was a time," he declared, "when God may have overlooked man's ignorance, but that time has passed. He now commands all people everywhere to repent and turn from their sins to Him. For He has set a day when He will judge the entire earth by the Man He has appointed. He has proven that this Man is worthy by raising Him from the dead."

When the magistrates heard Paul talking about Christ's resurrection, they mocked him. Some, however, wanted to hear more, and a few followed him and became believers.

Two Representative Sermons

Paul's sermon in Athens is the second time in Acts that Luke gives a detailed summary of the apostle's message. The first time was in Pisidian Antioch and is recorded in Acts 13:14-41. As you may remember, we discussed that sermon on Day 25. (You may want to review that lesson at this time.)

By comparing these two sermons of Paul, we can learn some valuable lessons about preaching the gospel. We especially learn how we can adapt our messages to different audiences in different cultural contexts. Let's now look at three of those lessons:

Always Be Ready

First, we learn that we must be ready to preach the gospel any time an opportunity presents itself—even in different cultural contexts. When Paul was invited to preach in the synagogue in Antioch, he was ready. Later, when he was invited to preach on Mars Hill in Athens, he was again ready. Paul later reminded Timothy, his son in the faith, that he should be prepared to preach the word of God "in season and out of season" (2 Tim. 4:2). In other words, he should be prepared to preach the gospel in any circumstance.

How can we be ready to preach the gospel in any circumstance? Like Paul, we must remain full of the Holy Spirit and focused on our God-given mission.

Day 33: Paul Preaches in Athens

Know How to Adapt

We learn a second lesson from comparing Paul's two sermons in Pisidian Antioch and Athens. If we, like Paul, want to effectively communicate Christ in varying cultural contexts, we must know how to adapt our method and our message to fit our given audience.

Paul's approach in Antioch was much different from his approach in Athens. In Antioch, he entered the Jewish synagogue and sat down to teach them. In Athens, he went to Mars Hill, stood to his feet, and addressed his audience. In each case, Paul was adapting his style of delivery to local cultural expectations.

Also, in his sermon in Antioch, Paul had much to say about the history of Israel. He talked about Moses and about how Jesus had descended from King David. He further noted how Jesus' coming was a fulfillment of Old Testament prophecies. These things were important to Jews.

However, in Athens Paul proceeded differently. There, he did not discuss Israel's past, for his audience knew nothing about Jewish history. He rather talked about Greek culture and religion. He called attention to the Athenian's worship, and referred to their monument to the "Unknown God." He even quoted one of their pagan poets. He did these things to identify with the culture of Athens.

In our preaching today, we too should know our audience. We should be aware of their customs. And we should look for stories from their cultures that can illustrate biblical truth. In this way, we can help them to better understand the message of Christ. The better we understand a people's culture, the better we will be able to communicate the message of Christ to them.

Day 33: Paul Preaches in Athens

Never Compromise

We can learn a third lesson from comparing Paul's two sermons. While we should adapt our sermons to the culture of the audience, we should never compromise the message of gospel. In both Antioch and Athens Paul proclaimed Christ. He boldly declared that Jesus died on the cross and rose on the third day. He further called on the people to repent of their sins and put their faith in Christ alone for salvation. Paul knew that Jesus was the only way for people to be reconciled to God. He would later write, "There is one God and one mediator between God and mankind, the man Christ Jesus" (1 Tim. 2:5). Like Paul, we must never compromise the message of the gospel.

Day 33: Paul Preaches in Athens

Day 34

Successful Ministry in Corinth

Acts 18:1-28

One reason many pastors and church planters leave the ministry is that they become discouraged. In today's story from the Book of Acts, even the great apostle Paul becomes discouraged. However, the Lord helps him to overcome his discouragement and continue in the work.

Leaving Athens, Paul traveled westward to Corinth, the provincial capital of Achaia. Corinth was a large city of about 500,000 inhabitants. It was known for its gross immorality.

Every Sabbath Paul went to the city's synagogue and tried to persuade the Jews and Greeks to follow Christ. One such Sabbath he met a Jewish man named Aquila and his wife Priscilla. They had recently come from Rome. Since they were tentmakers like him, they invited him to stay in their home and work with them. They also ministered with Paul, helping him to plant the church in Corinth. Later Paul mentions that Priscilla and Aquila not only ministered with him, they risked their lives for him (Rom. 16:3-4).

In Corinth some of the Jews began to openly oppose Paul, casting insults at him. Finally, he removed his outer clothes, and in front of

Day 34: Successful Ministry in Corinth

everyone, shook the dust from them. "Your blood be on your own heads," he said, "I am clear of my responsibility. From now on I will go to the Gentiles" (v. 6).

Paul then left the synagogue and went next door to the home of one Titius Justus, a God-fearing Gentile man. Soon, Crispus, the ruler of the synagogue, and his entire family believed in the Lord. Many other Corinthians also believed and were baptized. Eventually things became so tense that Paul began to fear for his safety.

One night the Lord Jesus appeared to him in a vision and said, "Don't be afraid, but keep on speaking, for I am with you and I will not allow anyone to harm you. I have many people in this city." Paul then took heart and stayed in Corinth for another year and a half teaching the word of God.

One day some rowdy Jews got together and seized Paul. They hauled him before Gallio, the provincial governor and accused him saying, "This fellow tries to persuade people to worship God in ways that are contrary to our law."

Just as Paul was about to answer their charges, Gallio butted in. Motioning to the Jews, he said, "Look here! You men have no real case. This man has committed no crime. This is just another one of your religious disputes, another pointless argument over names and words. I refuse to get involved in such matters. Take care of it yourselves."

This so angered the Jews that they turned on Sosthenes, the leader of the synagogue. They grabbed the poor man and began to beat him right there in the courtroom. Gallio, however, turned away and paid no attention to what was happening.

After that, Paul remained in Corinth for quite a while. He then sailed for Syria with Priscilla and Aquila.

Day 34: Successful Ministry in Corinth

On their way, the three missionaries had a stopover in Ephesus While there, Paul reasoned with the Jews in the synagogue. He needed to leave, so he left Priscilla and Aquila to lead the new church they had planted.

Meanwhile, a man named Apollos came to Ephesus from Alexandria, Egypt. He was a learned man and a gifted preacher. He knew the Old Testament Scriptures quiet well, and he taught the truth about Jesus. However, he had only experienced the baptism of John the Baptist.

When Priscilla and Aquila discovered this, they invited Apollos into their home. There they taught him that Jesus was the Christ and the baptizer in the Holy Spirit, as John himself had taught (Luke 3:16). Later, when Apollos went to Corinth, God used him in powerful ways.

From the story of Paul's missionary work in Corinth, we learn two important ministry lessons. Also, from the story of Priscilla and Aquila's ministry in Ephesus we learn a third important lesson.

Rely on the Spirit

First, from Paul's ministry in Corinth we learn of the importance of a Spirit-empowered church planting strategy. When Paul arrived in Corinth, he came with such a plan. It involved two key elements: first, he would focus on proclaiming the message of the cross, and second, he would minister in the power of the Spirit.

In Athens, Paul had tried to convince the residents to turn to Christ by using superior wisdom and philosophy. Yet, his results were small. In Corinth, however, "Paul devoted himself exclusively to preaching, testifying…that Jesus was the Christ" (v. 5).

Day 34: Successful Ministry in Corinth

Paul talks more about this Corinthian strategy in a letter he later wrote to the church. In that letter Paul told them that, en route to their city, he had resolved to preach nothing except "Jesus Christ and him crucified." He further reminded them, "My message and my preaching were not with wise and persuasive words, but with a demonstration of the Spirit's power" (1 Cor. 2:2-4).

We would be wise to do the same in our evangelism and church planting efforts today. We must be vigilant to preach Christ and Christ alone. And we must do all in the power and anointing of the Holy Spirit.

Trust the Lord

We learn a second valuable lesson from the story of Paul's missionary work in Corinth. We learn how we can always trust the Lord to encourage us in our times of trial. In Corinth, Paul ministered in the face of threats and opposition. Because he knew that the Lord was with him, however, he was able to endure.

When Jesus was commissioning His disciples, He promised them, "Surely I am with you always, to the very end of the age" (Matt. 28:20). Paul knew that to be true. What's more, when things became particularly difficult for Paul, the Lord appeared to him in a night vision. Jesus himself encouraged Paul to continue with his ministry there.

We can count on the Lord to do the same for us today. When we go out to preach the gospel, we like Paul, should go in the power of the Spirit. And we should focus our preaching and teaching on "Christ and him crucified." Then, when difficult times come, we can trust that the Lord to come to us with words of encouragement.

Sometimes He may appear in a vision. At other times, He will speak directly by His Spirit to our spirits. Such times of encouragement most often come when we are seeking the Lord's face in prayer.

Encourage the Women

Finally, from the account of Priscilla and Aquila's ministry in Ephesus we learn a third important ministry lesson. This story teaches us that God calls and uses women as well as men. This husband and wife team had ministered in Rome and they had helped Paul plant the church in Corinth (vv. 2, 8). Later, they shared an effective pastoral ministry in Ephesus (v. 26). Paul called them his "fellow workers in Christ Jesus" (Rom. 16:3).

Sometimes women minister hand-in-hand with their husbands. At other times God calls them to minister alone. Whatever the case, we should always encourage women in the ministry to which God has called them.

Day 34: Successful Ministry in Corinth

Day 35

The Ephesian Outpouring

Acts 19:1-7

Church planters often make one of two mistakes. Some go to the work full of the Holy Spirit but without a clear plan. Others have a plan, but their plan does not include the empowering of the Spirit. When Paul arrived in Ephesus, however, he came in the power of the Holy Spirit—and he had a well-devised plan. It was a plan that he had received from the Lord Jesus himself.

Paul concluded his second missionary journey by returning to Antioch, Syria, where the journey had begun. After spending some time there, he set out on his third journey.

He first revisited the churches he had planted in Galatia and Phrygia. He then ventured westward across the breadth of Asia Minor until he arrived at Ephesus, the provincial capital of Asia. Ephesus was a great city of about 750,000 inhabitants. It contained the famed Temple of Artemis, one of the Seven Wonders of the Ancient World.

Soon after arriving in Ephesus, Paul encountered twelve disciples. These men were likely members of the city's emerging church. He abruptly asked them, "Did you receive the Holy Spirit when you believed?"

Day 35: The Ephesian Outpouring

They answered, "We've never even heard of the Holy Spirit."

"Then what baptism did you receive?" Paul responded.

They replied, "The baptism of John the Baptist."

Paul then explained, "John's baptism was a baptism of repentance. It pointed to faith in Jesus who was to come."

At that, Paul baptized the twelve Ephesian disciples into the name of the Lord Jesus. He then laid his hands on them, and the Holy Spirit came upon them, just as he had come upon the 120 at Pentecost and on the Gentiles in Caesarea. They began to speak in tongues and prophesy.

Paul then went to work. He took these twelve newly Spirit-baptized disciples and led them into the synagogue where he began to declare the kingdom of God. This continued for three months until some members of the synagogue began to complain. Paul then took the disciples and moved to the lecture hall of Tyrannus where, for the next two years, he taught them.

All the while, the Spirit of the Lord worked powerfully through Paul. God used him to heal diseased people and to deliver those who were bound by demonic spirits. He became so famous that even the demons knew his name, and many people turned to the Lord.

Some of those who became Christians denounced their former lives by publicly burning the fetishes they had used to practice sorcery. As a result, the word of the Lord continued to spread powerfully throughout the region.

Of course, the devil wasn't happy with this development, so he began to fight back. He used a silversmith named Demetrius to incite a great riot in the city. This man was angry because Paul was hurting his business. He sold little silver shrines to the people, which they used in the worship of Artemis.

Demetrius went into the public square and began to cry out, "These men are insulting our great goddess. They are causing many people to turn away from her by saying that manmade gods are no gods at all. We must put a stop this madness!"

This so inflamed the people that they began to chant over and over, "Great is Artemis of the Ephesians!" This went on for two hours. Finally, the city clerk was able to quiet them down. After scolding them, he sent them to their homes.

The Twelve Disciples

Who were the twelve disciples that Paul found when he arrived in Ephesus? Some have taught that these men were not true disciples of Jesus; they were merely followers of John the Baptist. However, this idea is not correct. These men were true Christians and were likely members of the city's emerging church. We know this because, in Luke's gospel and in Acts, every time he uses the word disciple without any qualifying adjective, he is talking about disciples of Christ.

Although these twelve men had been born again, they had not yet been baptized in the Holy Spirit and thus empowered as Christ's witnesses. Paul knew that, if they were to be effective witnesses for Christ, they would need the Spirit's power.

The same is true for us today, if we are to be effective witnesses, we, too, must be clothed with the Spirit's power.

The Seventh Key Outpouring

The outpouring of the Holy Spirit on the twelve disciples in Ephesus is the seventh and last key outpouring of the Holy Spirit in

Day 35: The Ephesian Outpouring

Acts. You may remember that, in this study, we have already looked at six outpourings of the Spirit in Acts. These are

- Pentecost (Acts 2:1-4),
- the Second Jerusalem Outpouring (4:31),
- the Samaritan Outpouring (8:15-17),
- the Damascus Outpouring (9:17-18),
- and the Caesarean Outpouring (10:44-46).

Now, in this lesson, we observe a seventh key outpouring of the Spirit. We call this outpouring the Ephesian Outpouring. As with the previous six outpourings in Acts, this outpouring results in powerful missionary witness. Also, as with the previous six outpourings, it demonstrates Luke's empowerment-witness motif discussed on Day 1 of this study.

This pattern was first presented in Acts 1:8, where Jesus said, "But you will receive power when the Holy Spirit comes on you; and you will be my witnesses in Jerusalem, and in all Judea and Samaria, and to the ends of the earth." This repeated pattern reveals Luke's primary reason for writing Acts. He wanted to call the church back to its Pentecostal and missionary roots.

The Spirit is doing the same today. He is empowering believers to be Christ's witnesses to the lost. If we will be empowered by the Spirit and remain committed to God's mission, we too can become powerful witnesses for Christ.

The Normative Results

When Paul laid hands on the twelve disciples "the Holy Spirit came on them, and they spoke in tongues and prophesied" (v. 6). This same thing happened when the Spirit came on the 120 at Pentecost in Acts 2 and the Gentiles in Caesarea in Acts 10.

Day 35: The Ephesian Outpouring

According to Luke's teaching in Acts, one can expect two results when he or she is baptized in the Holy Spirit. First, they will speak in tongues as the Spirit gives utterance. This is the "initial physical evidence" or "normative missional sign" that one has been baptized in the Holy Spirit. Second, they will become Spirit-empowered witnesses. This is the "functional result" and main purpose of one's being baptized in the Holy Spirit.

The same is true today. When one is baptized in the Holy Spirit, he or she will speak in tongues as the Spirit enables them, and they will become powerful witnesses for Christ. Thus, as leaders in Christ's church, we must ensure that we ourselves have been empowered by the Holy Spirit. We must further ensure that every member in our church has been baptized in the Spirit and mobilized as Christ's witness to the lost. Then, together, we should go out and tell others about Jesus.

Day 35: The Ephesian Outpouring

Day 36

The New Testament Strategy of the Spirit

Acts 19:1-10

The missionary arrived by airplane. The pastor of the church where he was to minister picked him up at the airport. As they were driving through the heart of the great city, the missionary asked, "Pastor, what is your strategy for reaching this city for Christ?" The pastor was embarrassed and had to admit that he had no real plan for reaching his city. In fact, he had never even thought about such a thing.

In the Book of Acts, however, when the apostle Paul arrived in Ephesus, he had a well-developed strategy for reaching the city—and all of Roman Asia—with the gospel. In this lesson we will look at that strategy. We call it the New Testament "Strategy of the Spirit." You will remember that, yesterday, we examined the Ephesian Outpouring. Today, we will examine Paul's Ephesian Campaign and the strategy he used to carry it out.

Day 36: The New Testament Strategy of the Spirit

A Clear Goal

Every good strategy begins with a clear goal. On arriving in Ephesus, Paul's goal was to strengthen and mobilize the emerging church in the city. He would then use that church to scatter other Spirit-empowered missionary churches throughout the Roman province of Asia. We know this because Luke says that, after Paul had been in Ephesus for only two years, "all the Jews and Greeks who lived in the province of Asia heard the word of the Lord" (v. 10).

But, how did Paul accomplish this? The preceding nine verses tell us what Paul did to achieve this goal. Those verses reveal the three pillars of Paul's strategy:

- Holy Spirit empowering,
- Spirit-empowered witness, and
- mobilizing workers.

Let's look at how Paul implemented each part of his strategy.

Pillar One: Empowering

The first pillar of Paul's Ephesian strategy was the empowering of the Holy Spirit. Paul himself entered the city full of the Holy Spirit. Because of this, he was able to proclaim the gospel with power, pray with others to be filled with the Spirit, and be used by God to heal the sick and cast out demons.

Paul understood, however, that it was not enough for him alone to be full of the Spirit. If the work was to prosper, the church he was seeking to mobilize would need to be Spirit-empowered too. So when he arrived in Ephesus and discovered twelve disciples, he immediately asked them, "Did you receive the Holy Spirit when you believed?"

Paul asked them this question because he wanted to know if they were spiritually ready to help him in his mission of reaching Ephesus and Asia Minor with the gospel. He knew that, if they were to be effective witnesses, they too would need to be empowered by the Holy Spirit.

When "he placed his hands on them, the Holy Spirit came on them, and they spoke in tongues and prophesied" (v. 7). Thus empowered, the church in Ephesus would become a powerful center of missionary activity. It would reach into every corner of the province.

Today, we must follow Paul's example. When leading our churches into any evangelistic, church planting, or missions outreach, we must ensure that, as leaders, we are full of the Holy Spirit and moving in His power. We must further ensure that those who participate in the outreach are full of the Spirit.

This fullness of the Spirit comes from an experience Jesus called the baptism in the Holy Spirit (1:4-8). It is maintained through prayer and openness to the Spirit (Luke 11:9-13).

Pillar Two: Spirit-empowered Witness

The second pillar of Paul's missionary strategy was Spirit-empowered witness. Like the first pillar, this one also has two parts. It involves anointed proclamation of the gospel and demonstrations of kingdom power through the manifestation of signs and wonders.

Once the twelve disciples had been empowered by the Holy Spirit, Paul immediately took them into the synagogue. There, he "spoke boldly for three months, arguing persuasively about the kingdom of God" (v. 8). In others words, Paul boldly proclaimed that Jesus the Messiah, had come to set up His kingdom on earth.

Paul also witnessed by performing signs and wonders by the power of the Spirit. The Bible says that "God did extraordinary miracles through Paul" (v. 11). These miracles included healing the sick and casting out demons. As a result, "the word of the Lord spread widely and grew in power" (v. 20).

Today we should follow Paul's example. We must faithfully proclaim the gospel of Jesus Christ in the power of the Holy Spirit. Then, we must trust God to confirm His word by performing miraculous signs and wonders. We can then expect the word of the Lord to spread widely and many people to come to know Christ.

Pillar Three: Mobilizing Workers

The third pillar of Paul's missionary strategy was mobilizing workers. Like the previous two pillars, this one also had two parts, training workers and sending them to the work.

Once the disciples had been empowered by the Spirit, Paul began training them for regional missions. Luke says, "He took the disciples with him and had discussions daily in the lecture hall of Tyrannus" (v. 9). In other words, he started a school for training workers. In this school, he must have taught them the basics of the gospel. He also likely taught them church planting and missions strategy.

Then, Paul began sending the disciples out into every corner of the province to preach the gospel and plant churches. No doubt, they employed the same missionary strategy as Paul. They preached with power and planted Spirit-empowered missionary churches. The application of this strategy resulted in a spontaneous multiplication of churches throughout the entire region. As a result, "all the Jews and Greeks who lived in the province of Asia heard the word of the Lord" (v. 10).

The New Testament Strategy of the Spirit

Paul's strategy for Ephesus and Asia Minor was not original with him. He was simply following the example of Jesus. Jesus mobilized His disciples by training them and sending them out. As they went, they were to preach the gospel and to demonstrate its power with signs following. However, before they did any of this, they were to wait in Jerusalem to be empowered by the Holy Spirit. Paul was simply "working the plan." He was following the example of Jesus in sending His church into the world.

We, as ministers of the gospel, must do the same. We must approach our work with a well thought out, biblically-based strategy. Everything we do must be focused. We must intentionally plant Spirit-empowered missionary churches. To do this, we must ensure that we are full of the Holy Spirit. We must further ensure that our church members have been empowered by the Spirit. Only then will these believers have the zeal and power needed to spread the gospel to the surrounding areas.

Further, we must preach the gospel in the power of the Spirit and expect Christ to confirm His word with signs following. Finally, we must carefully mobilize the churches we plant for further missional ministry. We can do this through focused training and by sending and supporting those who have been trained.

Day 36: The New Testament Strategy of the Spirit

Day 37

A Final Farewell

Acts 20:1-38

Someone has said, "Saying goodbye is most painful when you know you'll never say hello again." That's how the Ephesian elders must have felt in today's story from the Book of Acts.

Paul's ministry in Ephesus continued for three years. Leaving there, he and his companions traveled through Macedonia and Greece proclaiming the good news and encouraging the disciples. They eventually arrived at Troas.

The following Sunday Paul met with the disciples there in an upper room. In the gathering was a young man named Eutychus who was sitting in an open window. As Paul taught late into the night, Eutychus fell asleep and tumbled to the ground below. Paul rushed down and found the young man dead. So, he took him in his arms and held him. Then, turning to the people he announced, "Don't be alarmed. He's alive!" God had healed him, and everyone rejoiced at what He had done.

The next day, Paul set out for Jerusalem. He wanted to be there for Pentecost. On their way, he and his missionary party passed through Miletus, a port city about 45 miles (75 kilometers) south of

Day 37: A Final Farewell

Ephesus. From there Paul sent a message to the elders of the church at Ephesus, asking them to come and meet with him.

When they arrived, Paul spoke from his heart, reminding them of how he had lived among them. "I served the Lord humbly and with tears," he said, "and I never failed to proclaim the good news to all people, telling them that they must turn to God, repent of their sins, and put their faith in the Lord Jesus."

He then told them of his plans: "Now, the Spirit is urging me to go to Jerusalem. He has revealed to me that I will suffer pain and imprisonment there. However, such things do not move me. My one desire is to finish the race the Lord Jesus has given me. I must complete my work of telling people about God's grace."

Then, turning to look them in the face, he said, "I know that you will never see me again. Therefore, I declare to you, I am innocent of the blood of all people. For not once did I shrink from teaching you the whole will of God."

Paul then charged the elders, "Guard yourselves and the flock of God. Never forget that God purchased them with His own blood, and that the Holy Spirit has appointed you to watch over them. You are to protect them from savage wolves who will come in and try to lead them from the truth."

"Now," he said, "I entrust you to the grace of God, and I remind you how I selflessly labored among you. I even worked with my own hands to provide for my fellow workers and myself. I have coveted no man's silver or gold or clothing."

He concluded his message by saying, "Remember the words of the Lord Jesus. He said, 'It is more blessed to give than to receive.'"

Day 37: A Final Farewell

When Paul finished speaking, they all knelt down together and prayed. Some of the elders began to cry, for they knew that they would never see Paul's face again. Paul then embraced them all and bid them farewell. Together they walked down to where the ship was waiting.

Paul's address to the Ephesian elders is his third extended speech in Acts. You may remember that the first one took place in Pisidian Antioch during Paul's first missionary journey. The second occurred in Athens, during his second journey. Now, this third speech takes place in Ephesus during Paul's third and final journey.

This speech, however, is different from the first two. The first two were sermons where Paul proclaimed the gospel to the lost. However, in this address to the Ephesian elders, Paul speaks as brother to brother. In this moving speech, the aging apostle opens his heart and challenges his friends and colleagues in ministry to continue in the work of the Lord. In it we sense Paul's love for the brethren and his single-minded commitment to Christ and His mission.

From Paul's final instructions to the Ephesian elders, we learn three important lessons about our responsibilities as pastors and church leaders:

Guard the Flock of God

First, we learn that, as pastors and church leaders, we must guard the flock of God. Paul charged the Ephesian elders, "Keep watch over yourselves and all the flock of which the Holy Spirit has made you overseers. Be shepherds of the church of God, which he bought with his own blood" (v. 28).

We must never forget that the people do not belong to us. They belong to God, and to Christ who purchased them with His own blood. We are simply Christ's under shepherds and caretakers of the flock of God. As such, we must love them and protect them from "savage wolves [who] will come in...and will not spare the flock" (v. 29). We must never forget that God will someday judge us on how we cared for His sheep (see Jer. 23:1-2; James 3:1).

Faithfully Proclaim the Gospel

Secondly, as Christ's under shepherds, we must faithfully proclaim the gospel to all. Paul reminded the Ephesian elders, "You know that I have not hesitated to preach anything that would be helpful to you, but... I have declared to both Jews and Greeks that they must turn to God in repentance and have faith in our Lord Jesus" (vv. 20-21).

Our primary responsibility as ministers of the gospel is to proclaim Jesus to all. We must tell them that He died on the cross for their sins and was raised on the third day. We must further tell them that they must repent of their sins, put their faith in Christ alone for salvation, and follow Him. If they will do this, God will forgive them of their sins and give to them eternal life. Woe to that pastor or church leader who fails to preach the gospel.

Teach the Whole Will of God

Finally, as keepers of God's flock, we must teach the people the "whole will of God." Paul told the Ephesian elders, "I declare to you today that I am innocent of the blood of all men. For I have not hesitated to proclaim to you the whole will of God" (vv. 26-27).

So, not only must we proclaim the gospel, we must teach all the great truths of Scripture. Jesus commanded His disciples to "go into all the world and preach the good news to all creation" (Mark 16:15). He also charged them to "make disciples of all nations...teaching them to obey everything I have commanded you" (Matt. 28:19-20).

Day 37: A Final Farewell

We do this by systematically teaching the word of God to the people of God. By doing this, we protect them from "savage wolves [who will come and] distort the truth in order to draw away disciples after them" (vv. 29-30).

Every pastor should ensure that there is systematic teaching of the word of God in his or her church—and they should personally oversee and participate in that process.

Day 37: A Final Farewell

Day 38

To Jerusalem: Journey, Arrival, and Arrest

Acts 21:1-36

In God's work, we are sometimes called to lead. At other times, we are called to follow. Most often, we are called to do both at the same time. Whether leading or following, we must do so with grace and humility. In today's lesson, we see Paul leading his missionary team to Jerusalem. Then, when he arrived in the city, he humbly submitted himself to the leaders of the Jerusalem church. As a result, God's will was done, and His kingdom was advanced.

Leaving Miletus, Paul and his team continued on their journey to Jerusalem. They travelled as far as Caesarea, where God had first poured out his Spirit on the Gentiles. There, Philip the evangelist welcomed them into his home. Philip was one of the seven deacons who, years before, was chosen to care for the Grecian widows in Jerusalem. By now, he had four unmarried daughters who prophesied.

Soon after their arrival in Caesarea, a prophet named Agabus arrived from Judea. He approached Paul, slid the apostle's belt from around his waist, and tied his own hands and feet. Then he said, "The

Day 38: To Jerusalem: Journey, Arrival, and Arrest

Holy Spirit says, 'This is how the Jews of Jerusalem will bind Paul. They will then hand him over to the Gentiles.'"

When the brothers and sisters heard this, they begged Paul not to go to Jerusalem. Paul replied, "My dear friends, why are you weeping? You are breaking my heart. Not only am I ready to be jailed in Jerusalem, I am ready to die for Jesus' sake." Seeing how determined Paul was, the people gave up, saying, "The Lord's will be done."

Paul and his colleagues then proceeded to Jerusalem. When they arrived, the brothers welcomed them warmly. The next day Paul met with James and the elders of the church. Paul gave them a detailed report of all that God had done among the Gentiles through his ministry. When they heard this, they shouted, "Praise the Lord!"

The brothers then asked Paul if he would be willing to join some local Jewish brothers in observing certain purification rites in the temple. This would help the Jewish believers in Jerusalem know that Paul was not teaching those Jews who were becoming Christians that they must forsake their Jewish heritage.

Paul agreed to the plan. So the next day he purified himself and went with the men into the temple. On the seventh day of the rite, some Jews from Asia saw Paul in the temple complex. They grabbed him and started shouting, "Men of Israel, listen up. This man is leading people away from Judaism all over the world. He blasphemes this temple, and now he has defiled it by bringing in unclean Gentiles." Previously, they had seen Paul in the city with a Gentile and assumed that he had brought this man into the temple.

This false claim rocked the whole city, and many people rushed into the temple. They seized Paul and dragged him outside, slamming the temple gates behind them. They then began to pound Paul with their fists. If some Roman soldiers had not rescued him, they would have beaten him to death.

The commander of the garrison ordered that Paul be bound with chains. Then, he asked Paul, "What have you done to incite such an uproar?"

Overhearing this, the crowd began to shout one thing then another. They became so worked up that the soldiers had to lift Paul off his feet and carry him away. The mob followed and kept shouting, "Kill him! Kill him!" As they were about to enter the barracks, Paul asked the commander, "Will you allow me to speak to the people?" Seeing that the crowd had calmed down a bit, the commander agreed.

In the next lesson, we will examine what Paul said to the crowd. For now, let's look at the actions of Paul in today's story. From them we can learn three valuable ministry lessons:

Led by the Spirit

The first lesson we learn from Paul's actions is that we must be led by the Spirit of God. Paul was directed by the Spirit to go to Jerusalem. He told the Ephesian elders, "The Holy Spirit is compelling me to go to Jerusalem" (Acts 20:22). Throughout his ministry, Paul was guided by the Spirit. During Paul's second missionary journey, the Holy Spirit had directed him to go to Macedonia. Now, the Spirit had told him to go to Jerusalem.

The leadership of the Spirit is a key theme in Acts. Luke wants us to know that the Holy Spirit is the true Director of the work of missions. If we are going to be truly effective in missions work, we like Paul, must know how to hear the Spirit's voice. Then, when the Spirit does speak, we must be quick to obey. Paul wrote, "Those who are led by the Spirit of God are the children of God" (Rom. 8:1).

Day 38: To Jerusalem: Journey, Arrival, and Arrest

Submitted to Leadership

The second lesson we learn from Paul's actions in this story is that we must humbly submit ourselves to our spiritual leaders. When Paul arrived in Jerusalem, he immediately went to James and other church leaders. He did this to show his respect for them and to give a report of his work among the Gentiles.

In that meeting, the leaders asked him to participate in a Jewish purification ritual. On his own, Paul would have never done this. He believed that Christ had liberated him from practicing Jewish rituals. Years earlier, he wrote to the new Christians in Galatia and warned them against returning to Jewish rituals. He asked them, "Now that you know God…how is it that you are turning back to those weak and miserable principles? Do you wish to be enslaved by them all over again?" (Gal. 4:9-10). He then exhorted them to "stand firm" in the freedom that Christ had given them (5:1).

On this occasion, however, in order to help the leaders of the Jerusalem church resolve a pressing church problem, Paul graciously submitted himself to their leadership.

We should do the same. We should always show proper respect to those whom God has placed in spiritual leadership, and we should willingly submit ourselves to their authority. Ultimately, Paul's arrest in Jerusalem turned out for the best. Even though he was captured and imprisoned, his capture resulted in his going to Rome as God had intended.

Committed to the Mission

A third lesson we learn from Paul's actions in our story is that we must always remain committed to our God-given mission. As Paul moved steadily toward Jerusalem, the Spirit warned him that danger and imprisonment awaited him there. Many of his colleagues

Day 38: To Jerusalem: Journey, Arrival, and Arrest

interpreted this to mean that he was not to go to Jerusalem. Paul understood their fears; however, he also knew God's will. He was committed to fulfilling the mission Christ had given him. He told them, "I am ready not only to be bound, but also to die in Jerusalem for the name of the Lord Jesus." (v. 13).

Paul's chief ambition in life was to fulfill the ministry Christ had given him. He testified, "I consider my life worth nothing to me, if only I may finish the race and complete the task the Lord Jesus has given me—the task of testifying to the gospel of God's grace" (20:24).

Today, Christ has called us to make the same commitment to Him and His mission. "Be faithful, even to the point of death," He promises, "and I will give you the crown of life" (Rev. 2:10).

Day 38: To Jerusalem: Journey, Arrival, and Arrest

Day 39

Trials in Jerusalem

Acts 21:37-23:32

Have you ever been caught outside in a violent storm? You could feel the rain pounding and the wind whipping against you. That's a bit how Paul must have felt when the mob surrounded him in the temple courts in Jerusalem. Had it not been for the Roman soldiers, the rioters may have killed him.

Incited by some Jewish rabble-rousers, the unruly mob flooded into the temple courts. They wanted to get at the apostle Paul. The Roman soldiers, however, were able to keep them at bay. When the commander of the troop discovered that Paul was a Roman citizen, he gave him permission to address the crowd.

Paul began speaking to them in their own Jewish language. This caused the place to fall silent. Paul then reminded his hearers of how he too was once a zealous follower of the Law of Moses and a violent persecutor of the church.

Having gained their attention, Paul launched into the story of his conversion. He told how his life was transformed when he encountered the resurrected Christ on the Damascus Road. He then

Day 39: Trials in Jerusalem

told them how Jesus had commissioned him to preach the gospel to the Gentiles.

When the crowd heard Paul speak about the Gentiles, they were infuriated. They began tearing at their clothes and throwing dust into the air. Someone shouted, "Rid the earth of this man! He's not fit to live!" The commander also became caught up in the frenzy and ordered a centurion to flog Paul then interrogate him. But Paul surprised the centurion by asking, "Is it legal for you to flog a Roman citizen who hasn't even been found guilty?"

When the commander heard that Paul was a freeborn Roman citizen, he was alarmed and relented. Still, he kept Paul in chains.

The next day, the commander delivered Paul to a meeting of the Jewish high court, known as the Sanhedrin. They gave Paul permission to speak. He knew that the assembly was divided between Pharisees and Sadducees. So he began by saying, "My brothers, I am a Pharisee, the son of a Pharisee. I stand on trial because of my hope in the resurrection of the dead" (23:6).

When they heard this, the Pharisees (who believe in the resurrecttion) and the Sadducees (who do not believe in the resurrection) began yelling at each other. The assembly fell into such confusion that the commander once again had to order his soldiers to rescue Paul. They took him back to the barracks.

The next night, the Lord Jesus appeared to Paul and told him, "Take courage! As you have testified about me in Jerusalem, so you must also testify in Rome" (v. 11).

The next morning a group of about forty Jews hatched a plot against Paul. They bound themselves with an oath, vowing that they would neither eat nor drink until they had killed him. They told the Jewish rulers about their plan, asking for their help. As a ruse, the

Day 39: Trials in Jerusalem

chief priests and elders were to ask that Paul be brought before the Sanhedrin for questioning. The conspirators would then pounce on him and kill him on his way to the meeting.

Paul's nephew heard about the plot and told Paul. The apostle then called for his prison guard and had him take the boy to Claudius Lysias, the commander of the barracks. The boy told Lysias about the plot. That night, the commander had Paul transferred to Caesarea, escorted by a large detachment of soldiers. He wrote a letter to Felix, the governor of Judea, telling him of the situation. He stated that he had examined Paul and had found no charge against him deserving death or imprisonment.

Paul's Damascus Experience

In today's story, when Paul spoke to the crowd in Jerusalem, he told them how he had met Jesus on the road to Damascus. He will share this testimony again when he stands before King Agrippa.

Paul's experience in Damascus was significant, for there he had three life-changing encounters. First, he encountered the resurrected Christ, who transformed his life forever. Next, he encountered a disciple named Ananias who prayed with him and told him, "The God of our fathers has chosen you to know his will and to…be his witness to all men of what you have seen and heard" (22:14-15). Finally, Paul encountered the Holy Spirit who filled and empowered him to fulfil the mission that God had given him.

In the rest of the Book of Acts, Luke presents Paul as a man who ministered in the power of the Holy Spirit. Even when, at times, Luke does not say that Paul was full of the Spirit, we can rightfully assume that he is ministering in the Spirit's power.

With this in mind, let's take a moment to reflect on the empowering work of the Holy Spirit in the Book of Acts. You will remember that one of Luke's main purposes in writing Acts was to present the church a strategy for effective witness "to the ends of the earth." At the center of that strategy is the enabling work of the Holy Spirit. He is indeed the Superintendent of the Harvest! It is He who enables the church to fulfill its mandate to preach the gospel to all nations before Jesus comes again. He does this in at least three essential ways:

The Holy Spirit Inspires Mission

First, the Holy Spirit enables the church to fulfill God's mission by inspiring its members to get involved. He is ever working in believers' hearts to move them out of their places of comfort into His fields of service.

He did this with Peter. When the elders in Jerusalem asked him why he went to the Gentiles in Caesarea, Peter explained, "The Spirit told me to have no hesitation about going with them" (11:12).

The Spirit did the same thing in the church at Antioch. When the time came for the church to send out missionaries to the nations, the Holy Spirit moved in their midst. He told them, "Set apart for me Barnabas and Saul for the work to which I have called them" (13:2).

In the same way, the Holy Spirit will help us to mobilize the church today. We must ensure that our members are filled with the Spirit. And we must allow Him to move freely in our worship services. Then He will inspire our people to get involved in missions.

The Holy Spirit Empowers Mission

Another way the Holy Spirit enables the church to fulfill God's mission is by empowering Christians for witness. Jesus promised His disciples, "You will receive power when the Holy Spirit comes on you; and you will be my witnesses in Jerusalem, and in all Judea and Samaria, and to the ends of the earth" (1:8).

The Spirit empowers our witness in various ways. He inspires our teaching and preaching. He also gives us boldness and insight into the gospel and into the lives of those to whom we are ministering. As we preach the gospel, He manifests His presence through spiritual gifts, including confirming signs and wonders.

We, like the disciples before the Day of Pentecost, must faithfully wait until we have been "clothed with power from on high" (Luke 24:49).

The Holy Spirit Sustains Mission

A third way the Holy Spirit enables the church to fulfill God's mission is by encouraging workers who are hard at work in the field. In today's story, the Holy Spirit gave Paul a dream. In that dream the Lord stood near him and told him, "Take courage! As you have testified about me in Jerusalem, so you must also testify in Rome" (23:11). Because of this, Paul was encouraged to continue in his work.

As He did with Paul, Peter, and others, the Holy Spirit will come to us in our times of discouragement. He will comfort us through dreams, visions, and inner works of grace. As we seek the Lord's face, the Spirit will keep us focused on the mission of God. The Bible says that we can build ourselves up and keep ourselves in the love of God by praying in the Holy Spirit (Jude 20-21).

Day 39: Trials in Jerusalem

Day 40

Paul's Trials before Felix and Festus

Acts 23:23-25:12

Have you ever been insulted or falsely accused? If you have, you should rejoice, for Jesus said, "Blessed are you when people insult you, persecute you and falsely say all kinds of evil against you because of me. Rejoice and be glad, because great is your reward in heaven" (Matt. 5:11-12). He further said, "Bless those who curse you, pray for those who mistreat you" (Luke 6:28). In today's story from the Book of Acts, we see Paul putting these words of Jesus into action.

When Commander Claudius Lysias found out about the Jews' plot to assassinate Paul, he sent a contingent of soldiers to escort him to Caesarea. There, they handed Paul over to Felix, the Roman governor. Felix then ordered that the apostle be kept under guard in the palace of Herod.

When Ananias the high priest heard about this, he followed Paul to Caesarea. With him were some Jewish elders and a lawyer named Tertullus. There, they met with Felix who summoned Paul to appear before them. The Jews laid out their bogus charges, calling Paul "a

Day 40: Paul's Trials before Felix and Festus

ringleader of the Nazarene sect" (24:5). They further accused him of being a troublemaker and of trying to desecrate the temple.

When Paul was finally allowed to speak, he denied all the charges leveled against him. He did, however, confess faith in Christ. He said, "I admit that I worship the God of our fathers as a follower of the Way, which they call a sect." He further testified, "I have the same hope in God as these men, that there will be a resurrection of both the righteous and the wicked" (vv. 14-15). After listening to both sides, Felix decided not to rule on the case until he had heard from Lysias. He then ordered that Paul remain under guard.

Several days later, in a second meeting with Felix, Paul spoke to the governor about righteousness, judgment, and faith in Christ. As Felix listened, he grew more and more anxious. "That's enough for now!" he shouted. "I will send for you when I can find a more convenient time" (24:25). He then ordered that Paul be put in jail wanting to gain favor with the Jewish leaders. As the days passed, he often sent for Paul and talked with him, hoping to receive a bribe from him.

This went on for two years until Felix was replaced by Porcius Festus. Sensing an opportunity, the Jews went to Festus and asked that Paul be brought back to Jerusalem. They wanted to ambush him and kill him along the way. Festus, however, denied their request, saying, "You can come to Caesarea and press charges against him there."

Soon Festus convened a hearing in Caesarea. There, the Jews restated their false charges against Paul. Paul then made his defense. "I have done nothing wrong against the law of the Jews or against the temple or against Caesar," he said.

Day 40: Paul's Trials before Felix and Festus

When Festus asked Paul if he was willing to return to Jerusalem and stand trial there, Paul refused. "I am guilty of nothing deserving death," Paul said. "I am not afraid to die; however, I am innocent of all these trumped up charges. I will not go to Jerusalem. I appeal to Caesar!"

Hearing that Festus retorted, "You have appealed to Caesar. To Caesar you will go!"

A Follower of "the Way"

Before we look at some lessons we can learn from this story, let's look at a couple of insights.

The first insight has to do with a reference Paul made to the Christian faith. In making his defense before Felix and Festus, Paul said that he was a follower of "the Way." We do not often use the phrase today. However, in the Book of Acts, Luke uses it five times to describe Christianity.

The phrase reminds us of Jesus' words, "I am the way and the truth and the life" (John 14:6). It also suggests that being a Christian involves more than just accepting Christ as one's Savior. It is a way we must live, a path we must walk. In the Gospels, Jesus often commanded His disciples to "Follow me." He calls us to do the same today.

Paul's Appeal to Caesar

The second insight has to do with Paul's appeal to Caesar. When Festus asked him if he would be willing to go to Jerusalem to stand trial, Paul replied, "I appeal to Caesar!"

We must not, however, think of this appeal as an attempt by Paul to evade the charges against him. It was rather a Spirit-led move to ensure that he traveled to Rome, as Jesus in a night vision had said

Day 40: Paul's Trials before Felix and Festus

Paul must do (23:11). The Spirit had compelled Paul to go to Jerusalem (20:22), now, He was compelling him to appeal to Caesar.

In today's story, when Paul spoke to Felix about faith in Christ, the governor was deeply moved and became fearful. Earlier in Acts, when Peter was preaching on the Day of Pentecost, his listeners were "cut to the heart" (2:37).

From these two incidents, we can learn three important lessons about how we can persuade people to follow Christ:

Share the Gospel

First, we persuade people to follow Christ by sharing the gospel with them. In our story, when Paul spoke to Felix about righteousness, judgment, and faith in Christ, the governor's heart was stirred.

The gospel is more than words. Jesus once compared it to a seed that takes root and creates new life in the hearts of those who hear it. Paul wrote, "I am not ashamed of the gospel, because it is the power of God for the salvation of everyone who believes" (Rom. 1:16). The gospel has power to produce faith in the heart of the hearer.

We must faithfully tell people about Christ, knowing that the gospel will produce fruit in their lives.

Be Filled with the Spirit

Second, we learn that we persuade people to follow Christ by being filled with the Spirit. Not only was Felix moved by Paul's words, he was moved by the Holy Spirit who empowered his words. Jesus said that, when the Holy Spirit comes, "he will convict the world of guilt in regard to sin and righteousness and judgment" (John 16:8).

Day 40: Paul's Trials before Felix and Festus

When Spirit-filled believers speak the word of the Lord, the Spirit empowers their words. He also works in the heart of the hearers convicting them of sin and drawing them to Christ.

If we will be filled with the Spirit and faithfully share the gospel with the lost, the Spirit will anoint our words and will work in the people's hearts, convicting them of sin and drawing them to Christ.

Live Like Christ

Finally, we persuade people to follow Christ by living Christlike lives. Felix was stirred, not only by the gospel, and by the Holy Spirit, but also by Paul himself. He was moved by Paul's life and character. Paul's accusers were liars; he was truthful. They were devious; he was plain spoken. Their hearts were filled with bitterness; his was full of love. Paul's Christlike attitude deeply affected Felix.

If we want to influence people to Christ, we too must seek to live Christlike lives.

Day 40: Paul's Trials before Felix and Festus

Day 41

Paul's Trial before Agrippa

Acts 25:13-26:32

I was once called to meet with the president of a country in Africa. I was excited, but nervous. I wanted to show him proper respect; however, I also wanted to witness to him about Christ. In today's story from the Book of Acts, Paul had a similar experience. He was called before Agrippa, king of Judea, and he was determined to tell him about Jesus.

When King Agrippa arrived in Caesarea with his wife Bernice, Festus went to him and told him of his dilemma. "I have listened to the charges against Paul," he told the king, "and I have found no legitimate crime with which to charge him. However, Paul has appealed his case to Caesar and must now go to Rome to stand trial. "So here then is my question, O King. What should I write in my letter to Caesar? What shall I say is Paul's crime?"

Agrippa replied, "Before I answer you, I'd like to hear for myself what Paul has to say." So, they arranged to meet with Paul the next day.

The following day, Paul offered his defense. He explained to the king that his "crime" was nothing more than believing that there

Day 41: Paul's Trial before Agrippa

would be a resurrection of the dead. He then told Agrippa how he had once persecuted the church, and how one day he had encountered the risen Lord. "I was on my way to Damascus," he said, "when the Lord appeared as a blazing light from heaven, brighter than the noonday sun."

He continued, "The Lord told me that He had appointed me to be His servant and a witness of all that I had seen and heard. He said me, 'I am sending you to the Gentiles to open their eyes and to turn them from darkness to light, and from the power of Satan to God.'" Pausing for a moment, Paul said, "So then King Agrippa, I was not disobedient to the vision from heaven" (26:19).

The apostle concluded his defense: "I am saying nothing beyond what the prophets and Moses said would happen—that the Christ would suffer and, as the first to rise from the dead, would proclaim light to his own people and to the Gentiles" (26:22-23).

As Festus, who was with Agrippa, listened to Paul, he grew more and more restless. Then, suddenly he blurted out, "You are out of your mind, Paul! Your great learning is driving you insane" (v. 24).

This Paul denied. Then, turning to the king, he said, "King Agrippa, do you believe the prophets? I know you do."

Agrippa retorted, "Really Paul, do you think that can persuade me to be a Christian in such a short time?"

Paul replied, "Short time or long—I pray God that not only you, but all who are listening to me today, may become what I am, except for these chains" (vv. 28-29).

Having heard this, the king and his entourage left the room. After conferring with his advisers, Agrippa announced his decision. "This man has done nothing deserving of death or imprisonment," he said.

Day 41: Paul's Trial before Agrippa

Then, turning to Festus, he whispered, "He could have been set free if he hadn't appealed to Caesar."

Called as Servants

In this story, Paul told Agrippa that Jesus had appointed him "as a servant and as a witness" of the things he had seen (26:16). What was true for Paul is true for us today. Christ has also appointed each of us as His servant and His witness. Let's look more closely at each of these sacred duties.

First, Jesus has appointed us as His servants. This means that He is our Lord, and we are His bondservants. In today's story, Paul tells Agrippa of his first meeting with Jesus. On that occasion, he completely submitted himself to Jesus, twice calling Him "Lord." In his letters, Paul often refers to Jesus as the "Lord Jesus Christ" and to himself as "a servant of the gospel" (Eph. 3:7; Col. 1:23).

To make Jesus our Lord is to surrender ourselves to Him and His plan for our lives. Today, far too many Christians view Christ merely as their source of personal blessing. They want Him to be their Savior and Provider, but refuse to acknowledge Him as Lord and Master. Jesus, however, demands that we unconditionally submit ourselves to Him. He said, ""If anyone would come after me, he must deny himself and take up his cross daily and follow me" (Luke 9:23).

Commissioned as Witnesses

Not only has Christ called us to be His servants, He has also commissioned us to be His witnesses. Jesus told Paul that He had appointed him as "a servant and as a witness" of what he had seen. Earlier, when Jesus commissioned the Twelve, He commanded them to "make disciples of all nations" (Matt. 28:19). He further told them

Day 41: Paul's Trial before Agrippa

that they would be His witnesses "in Jerusalem, and in all Judea and Samaria, and to the ends of the earth" (1:8).

In today's story, Paul further explains his commission from Jesus. He tells Agrippa that Jesus sent him to the Gentiles to do three things:

- to open their eyes to the truth of the gospel,
- to turn them from darkness to light and from the power of Satan to God, and
- to offer them forgiveness of sins, and a place among Gods people.

Paul then said, "I preached that they should repent and turn to God" (v. 20). Not only did Paul remain true to Christ, he remained true to his God-given mission and message. He faithfully preached about Christ's death and resurrection. He taught how, through faith in Jesus and repentance toward God, people could find life everlasting (20:21).

Today, we have been called to do the same. As Christ's bondservants, we must obediently submit ourselves to Him. And as Christ's witnesses we must proclaim His name to all.

Paul has now finished his trials in Jerusalem and Caesarea. He will soon be on his way to Rome. However, he will not go as he had previously expected. Rather than go as a freeman, he will go to Rome in chains. We will talk about his perilous journey in our next lesson.

Day 42

Perilous Journey to Rome

Acts 27:1-44

Someone once said, "You can tell a lot about a man by the way he *acts;* you can tell even more about him by the way he *reacts.*" In today's story we observe the apostle Paul both acting and reacting, and in both ways he bears witness to Christ.

The Roman soldiers escorted Paul and his companions down to the waterfront. There they put them on a large merchant ship bound for Rome. Altogether, there were 276 people aboard the ship. After many days of slow difficult sailing, they arrived at Fair Havens on the southern tip of the island of Crete. By that time, winter had arrived, and sea travel had become hazardous. Nevertheless, the ship's crew decided to venture to the nearby port city of Phoenix because it had a more suitable harbor in which to spend the winter.

Paul however, warned them, "Men, I perceive that our voyage is going to be disastrous. If we go, we will lose our ship and everything in it. We may even lose our lives!" The Roman sailors, however, chose to ignore Paul's warning. So, when a soft southerly wind began to blow, they weighed anchor and sailed off to the west, staying close into the island's shoreline.

Day 42: Perilous Journey to Rome

Suddenly a great storm arose, and a violent wind drove their ship out into the open sea. For several days, the crew fought to keep the ship afloat. To lighten the load they threw the cargo and tackle overboard. Finally, in despair they abandoned all hope of being saved.

That's when Paul called the crew and passengers together. Lifting his voice above the gale, he shouted, "Eat something. You will need your strength." He then chided the captain and crew. "You should have listened to my advice," he said. "If you had, you would have avoided this tragedy."

Paul then addressed everyone: "Now I tell you, put your trust in God. Last night an angel of the Lord came to me. He told me not to be afraid of dying in this storm, for I must stand before Caesar. He let me know me that the ship itself will be lost, but everyone on board will be saved." This word gave everyone the courage they needed to continue the struggle.

On the fourteenth night, the ship was driven toward an island and was about to run aground. When Paul saw some crewmembers trying to launch a lifeboat, he warned them, "Unless you stay with the ship, you will perish."

Later, as day was breaking, Paul again urged everyone to eat. "Just follow my instructions," he said, "and not one of you will lose a single hair from his head." He then gave thanks to God, and they ate together.

Then, through the fog, the ship's lookout spied a sandy beach in the distance. They decided to run the ship aground there. So, hoisting the foresail to the wind, they made for the shoreline. The ship struck a sandbar with a great jolt. The bow stuck fast, and the violent waves pounded the stern, breaking the boat into pieces.

Day 42: Perilous Journey to Rome

Seeing what was happening, the centurion began shouting, "Abandon ship! Abandon ship!" Everyone leaped overboard and made for land. In this way, everyone was saved just as Paul had predicted.

Paul's Witness on the Ship

Today's story occurs some thirty years after Paul's first encounter with Jesus on the Damascus Road. On that day, his life was forever changed. The great persecutor of the church became its passionate promoter. Throughout his life, Paul never missed an opportunity to tell others about Jesus. He faithfully proclaimed Christ in homes and in open markets, in Jewish synagogues and in pagan temples, in humble classrooms and in stately courtrooms, in palaces and in prisons.

In today's story, we again see Paul witnessing for Christ. However, he is now witnessing in a very different setting. He is prisoner on a Roman ship headed for Rome. There, he will stand trial for crimes he did not commit.

Let's look at two valuable lessons we can learn from how Paul conducted himself on this perilous journey to Rome:

Let the Spirit Speak

The first lesson we learn from Paul's actions on his journey to Rome is that we can witness for Christ by allowing the Spirit to speak through us. The Spirit had moved through Paul in the past when he was preaching the gospel, casting out demons, and healing the sick. However, those were not the only times the Spirit moved through him. Paul lived his life in constant communion with the Spirit.

When the captain and his crew decided to sail from Fair Havens to another port, the Spirit of the Lord again spoke to Paul. Paul then warned the sailors against moving the ship. "I perceive that the voyage will be disastrous," he said.

Later, when they were in the heart of the storm fighting for their lives, Paul again spoke to the crew. "Men," he said, "you should have listened to me and not have sailed from Crete. If you would have done this, you would have spared yourselves this damage and loss."

But, how could Paul have known this? How could he have known what would happen in the future? He knew it because the Spirit revealed it to him. Then, when he spoke, he spoke by the Spirit. God had given him a word of knowledge, one of the nine gifts of the Spirit spoken of in 1 Corinthians 12.

Today, God wants to do the same through us. He wants to speak words of love, encouragement, and warning to those around us. If we are to be used by God in this way, we, like Paul, must remain full of the Holy Spirit, and we must be open to His promptings. Then, when He gives us a word for others, we must speak it with courage and grace.

Let Your Life Speak

We learn a second lesson from Paul's actions in the storm. Not only are we to witness with our words, we are to witness by the way we conduct ourselves in tough situations.

In the middle of the storm, Paul testified, "I have faith in God!" He then demonstrated his faith by the way he reacted to the storm. When others panicked, he remained cool. He calmly took control of the situation. As a result, the people listened to him, and their lives were saved. Paul was able to do this because he trusted in God and listened to the voice of the Spirit.

Day 42: Perilous Journey to Rome

Paul's confession that "I have faith in God" was not an empty confession. It summed up the core of his life and ministry. Years earlier, he had written to the Christians in Galatia, "I have been crucified with Christ and I no longer live, but Christ lives in me. The life I live in the body, I live by faith in the Son of God, who loved me and gave himself for me" (Gal. 2:20). Paul's confession should be our confession: "I live by faith in the Son of God."

Finally, when time came for the sailors to run the ship aground and make for the shore, Paul urged everyone to eat. He "took bread, and gave thanks to God in front of them all" (27:36). Paul's giving of thanks served as a witness to those who heard his prayer. His confidence in God in this desperate situation encouraged the others to trust in God also.

How we act—or react—in trying circumstances will influence others. Paul's steadfast confidence in God encouraged others to trust in Him. If we act in confident faith, it will witness to others. They, too, will be encouraged to put their faith in God. However, if we react in fear and unbelief, others will be reluctant to trust in God. We witness to others, not only with our words, but also by the way we respond to life's problems.

Day 42: Perilous Journey to Rome

Day 43

Miraculous Ministry on Malta

Acts 28:1-10

Jesus did not command us to go into all the world and work miracles. He rather told us to go and preach the gospel. Nevertheless, He did promise that God would confirm the proclamation of His word with "signs following" (Mark 16:16). In today's story, God did just that. On the island of Malta, He used Paul to work miracles, which opened the people's hearts to the good news.

The storm drove Paul's ship onto a sandbar, where it stuck fast. The powerful wind and waves then battered the hapless boat breaking it into pieces. In desperation, everyone aboard jumped into the churning sea and made for the shore. Those who could, swam for their lives. The rest desperately clung to planks and floating debris and paddled their way to land. By God's grace, they all made it safely to shore.

Because it was wintertime and cold, everyone stood shivering on the beach. Seeing their plight, the kindly islanders built a huge bonfire. They invited everyone to gather around the fire to warm themselves. The survivors soon discovered that they had crashed on the small island of Malta, about 100 miles south of Italy.

Day 43: Miraculous Ministry on Malta

The fire began to wane, so Paul pitched in and helped gather brushwood. As he was placing some sticks on the fire, a poisonous snake appeared from under a log. It struck Paul, its fangs sinking deep into his hand. Paul jerked back, but the snake held on.

When the locals saw the serpent dangling from Paul's hand, they whispered among themselves, "This man must be a murderer. He may have escaped the sea, yet the gods are seeing that he gets his just deserts."

They watched him, expecting him to drop dead at any moment. However, when Paul shook the snake into the fire and suffered no ill effects, they changed their minds. "He must be a god," they exclaimed!

A man named Publius was the chief magistrate of the island. His estate was near where the ship had wrecked. He was a generous man and invited Paul and his companions to stay with him in his home. They remained with him for three days. While there, Paul found out that Publius' elderly father was suffering with dysentery and a raging fever. So, he went into the old man's room, laid his hands on him, and asked God to heal him. Miraculously, the man was healed.

Word of the miracle spread fast, and soon everyone on the island knew about it. They brought their sick friends and family members to Paul, and he healed them all. Because of this, the people showered Paul and his companions with honors. Then, when it was finally time for them to leave for Rome, the people gave them everything they would need for the trip. The islanders then bid them farewell and sent them on their way.

Although Luke does not state that Paul preached the gospel on the island of Malta, we can be assured that he did. We believe this because it was Paul's common practice to proclaim Christ everywhere

Day 43: Miraculous Ministry on Malta

he went. Also, from church history we learn that Paul and his colleagues planted a thriving church on the island of Malta. In fact, Malta became the first-ever Christian nation. We also learn from history that Publius, the chief magistrate of the island, eventually became a leader in the church and ardent proclaimer of Christ. He was martyred by the Roman Emperor Hadrian in A.D. 125.

From Paul's ministry on the island of Malta, we learn three important ministry lessons concerning how we may advance the gospel into new areas.

Look for Opportunities

First, we learn that, when we go into new areas to spread the good news, we should look for opportunities to meet people's needs. This is what Paul did. Once he discovered that Publius' father was ill, he immediately went to him and healed him. This act of mercy opened the door to further ministry throughout the island. It also opened the hearts of the people to receive the gospel.

Today, we can do the same as we go out to share the good news. Like Paul, we should be aware of people's needs, both physical and spiritual. Then, as the Spirit directs us, we should trust the Lord to anoint us to minister to those needs. Once people see our genuine concern for them, they will more likely receive us. They will also be more likely to open their hearts to receive the gospel.

Understand the People

We learn a second lesson from the story of Paul's ministry in Malta. When we go to a new place to preach the gospel, we should seek to understand the people's worldview. Their worldview is the unique way they look at the world and interpret the meaning of events. For instance, when the Maltese people saw the snake attach itself to Paul's hand, they assumed that their goddess, Justice, was punishing him for being a murderer. Then, when Paul shook the snake off and suffered no harm, they changed their minds. They thought that Paul himself was a god. They were interpreting these events out of their own worldview.

Paul, however, had a biblical worldview. He knew that there is only one true God and that He has revealed himself in Scripture. Paul showed the Maltese the truth by preaching Christ to them and by performing miracles in His name.

Today, when we go to new places to preach the gospel, we should be like Paul. We should be aware of, and sensitive to, the people's worldview. However, like Paul, we must never compromise the gospel to accommodate the people's beliefs. Rather, we must lovingly teach the truth about God as revealed in the Bible.

Minister in Power

A third lesson we learn from Paul's ministry in Malta is that we can trust the Lord to confirm the preached word with miraculous signs. On Malta, Paul prayed with many sick people and the Lord healed them. This was in accordance with Jesus' Great Commission. In it, He commanded us to "go into all the world and preach the good news to all creation" (Mark 16:15). He then promised, "And these signs will accompany those who believe: In my name they will drive out demons; they will speak in new tongues…they will place their hands on sick people, and they will get well" (vv. 17-18).

If we will obey Christ's command to go and preach the gospel, we can then claim His promise to perform miracles to confirm the word.

Day 44

Paul Preaches in Rome

Acts 28:11-31

I have a friend, who, although he is not a great orator, is one of the most effective witnesses I have ever known. This is because his life is focused on Jesus Christ. And he seldom passes up an opportunity to tell others about his Lord. In today's story from the Book of Acts, Paul does the same thing. He uses an unlikely opportunity to tell others about Christ.

The people of Malta showered Paul and his team with gifts and sent them on their way. Sailing northward the missionaries soon arrived at Puteoli, a city on the western coast of Italy. To their delight, they encountered some fellow Christians there and were permitted to spend a full a week with them. Then, they headed north on the road to Rome.

When the brothers and sisters in Rome got word that Paul and the others were coming, they sent out a welcoming party to meet them. Paul was deeply touched by this kind gesture, and his heart was so filled with joy that he began to thank God right there in the presence of everyone.

Day 44: Paul Preaches in Rome

Together, they all headed out for Rome. When they arrived, Paul was allowed to stay in his own private quarters where a soldier was assigned to guard him.

After three days, Paul called for some Jewish leaders to meet with him. When they came, he explained to them his situation. "Brothers," he said, "As you may have heard, I have been accused of crimes against our people and customs. However, none of this is true.

"In Jerusalem, I was arrested and handed over to the Romans. They thoroughly investigated all the charges the Jewish leaders levelled against me and determined that I had done nothing wrong. The Romans wanted to let me go. However, the Jews objected so strongly that I was forced to appeal to Caesar."

He concluded his speech by saying, "So, that's why I asked you to come and hear me out. I also wanted to explain to you why I am bound in these chains. It is because I believe in the hope of Israel."

The Jews answered, "Paul, this is the first time we've heard anything about you. We didn't even know you were coming to Rome. We must admit, however, everything we have heard about your Christian friends has been bad. We'd like to hear what you have to say about them." They then arranged to meet with Paul on another day.

When the appointed day arrived, a large number of people came to hear what Paul had to say. From morning to evening he taught them about the kingdom of God. Quoting the Scriptures, he sought to convince them that Jesus was the Messiah. Some were persuaded, but others were stubborn and refused to believe. The two groups began to argue with one another.

That's when Paul interrupted them and said, "The Holy Spirit was right when he said through the prophet Isaiah, 'You will be ever hearing but never understanding; you will be ever seeing but never perceiving. For this people's heart has become calloused; they hardly hear with their ears, and they have closed their eyes. Otherwise they might see with their eyes, hear with their ears, understand with their hearts and turn, and I would heal them'" (vv. 26-27).

Concluding his message, Paul looked at his Jewish visitors, and said, "Listen to me. This salvation from God is now being offered to the Gentiles, and unlike some of you, they will accept it!"

After that, Paul stayed for two years in his own rented house in Rome. During those days, he welcomed everyone who wanted to come and see him. When they did, he boldly proclaimed the kingdom of God to them and taught them about the Lord Jesus Christ—and no one tried to stop him.

The Hope of Israel

In today's story, Paul told the Jews in Rome that he was in chains because of "the hope of Israel." In using this phrase, Paul was speaking of the Jewish hope that someday the dead would be raised.

Weeks earlier, Paul had told the mob in Jerusalem, "I stand on trial because of my hope in the resurrection of the dead" (23:6). That hope was confirmed when God raised Jesus the Messiah from the dead. Paul told the Corinthians, "Christ has indeed been raised from the dead, the firstfruits of those who have fallen asleep.... For as in Adam all die, so in Christ all will be made alive" (1 Cor. 15:20-22). Because we have put our faith in Christ, we have hope of a resurrection to eternal life.

From Paul's ministry in Rome, we can learn four important guidelines for our preaching today:

Faithfully Proclaim the Gospel

First, we learn that we should faithfully proclaim the good news about Jesus regardless of our situation. Even though Paul was a prisoner in Rome, he still preached the gospel. He was not allowed to go out to preach, so he called others to come to him. When they came, he shared Christ with them.

We should do the same. No matter what happens to us, we must preach the good news. We must boldly walk through any open door, even if the door is only partially open. Like Paul in Rome, we should "make the most of every opportunity" (Eph. 5:16). We should always be prepared to preach the word "in season and out of season" (2 Tim. 4:2).

Use Scripture

Secondly, from Paul's ministry in Rome, we learn that, when we do preach or teach, we must base everything we say on Scripture. In Rome, Paul "tried to convince [the Jews] about Jesus from the Law of Moses and from the Prophets" (v. 23). In other words, Paul used Scripture to teach them about their Messiah, Jesus Christ. We must do the same today. We must always and only preach and teach what is written in the Bible, the word of God.

Announce the Kingdom

Third, from Paul's example in Rome, we learn that we must faithfully proclaim the kingdom of God. The Bible says that Paul "preached the kingdom of God and taught about the Lord Jesus Christ" (v. 31). Thus, the Book of Acts began with Jesus teaching about the kingdom of God (1:3), and it ends with Paul doing the same. The kingdom of God is thus the overarching theme of the entire book. To preach the kingdom of God is to tell people that Jesus the

Day 44: Paul Preaches in Rome

King has come to establish His rule in in the world and in the hearts of people.

Focus on Jesus

Finally, from today's story we learn that Jesus must remain the central theme of all our preaching. Not only did Paul preach about the kingdom of God, he "taught about the Lord Jesus Christ" (v. 31).

In the same way, our preaching must focus on Christ. We are to tell everyone that Jesus died on the cross for their sins, and that God raised Him from the dead. Then, we are to call on them to repent of their sins and put their faith in Christ alone for salvation.

That's how the Book of Acts ends. According to Jesus' prophecy in Acts 1:8, the gospel has been preached in the power of the Spirit in Jerusalem, and in all Judea and Samaria and then to much of the Roman world. Today the Savior's prophecy continues to be fulfilled as the church advances in the power of the Spirit to the ends of the earth.

In tomorrow's lesson we will review some powerful truths we should take from our study of Acts.

Day 44: Paul Preaches in Rome

Day 45

The Message of Acts

The story is told of an old Salvation Army soldier who stood at the grave of General William Booth, founder of the movement. As he pondered the powerful influence of Booth's life and ministry, he prayed, "Oh, Lord! Do it again!"

We have now come to the end of our study of the Book of Acts. In this study, we have learned many things. Most importantly, we have learned about God's mission. We have seen how the New Testament church went about fulfilling that mission in the power of the Holy Spirit. As we think about their wonderful deeds, we are inspired to pray, "Oh, Lord! Do it again!"

Hopefully, you have applied these lessons to your own ministry. And hopefully, you have personally experienced the power of the Holy Spirit in your life, just as the first Christians did in theirs.

As we conclude our study, we ask a final question: "What is the message of Acts for the church today?"

The Message of Acts

To answer that question, we must first answer another question. We addressed this question on Day 1 of our study. The question is "Why did Luke write the Book of Acts in the first place?"

Day 45: The Message of Acts

As you may remember, on Day 1 we learned that Luke wrote Acts with a clear purpose in mind. He wrote to call the church back to its Pentecostal and missionary roots. In Acts 1:8, Jesus promised, "You will receive power when the Holy Spirit comes on you; and you will be my witnesses in Jerusalem, and in all Judea and Samaria, and to the ends of the earth." This final promise of Jesus is the key to understanding the entire Book of Acts.

Luke wrote Acts about thirty years after the Day of Pentecost. He was thus writing to a second generation of Christians. These believers lived far away from Jerusalem, and they were likely suffering persecution. Because of this, they had lost much of their spiritual fervor and missionary zeal. In Luke's mind, these struggling disciples urgently needed to hear the story of the church's powerful beginning and irresistible missionary advance.

Luke further wrote to tell his readers about the baptism in the Holy Spirit. He wanted them to know that they could experience the same empowering as did Jesus and the early Christians. If they would do this, they too could become a powerful missionary force in their world. What's more, this could happen even in the midst of persecution.

This, then, is the message of Acts: Any church—or any disciple—can powerfully participate in Christ's mission to take the gospel to the lost. They must only commit themselves fully to Christ's mission and be powerfully filled with the Holy Spirit.

A Missions Strategy

Luke further wrote Acts as a manual for missions strategy. In its pages we have discovered the New Testament "Strategy of the Spirit" used by the Early Church. It was a strategy handed down to them by

Christ. It transformed a small group of disillusioned disciples in Jerusalem into a global missions force.

Just as some stools have three legs, this missions strategy has three parts. And, just as such a stool cannot stand if any leg is removed, this strategy will not work if any part is removed.

Empowering. The first leg of the New Testament Strategy of the Spirit is empowering. Jesus commanded His disciples to "Go into all the world and preach the good news to all creation" (Mark 16:15). But first, He said, "Stay in the city until you have been clothed with power from on high" (Luke 24:49). The disciples obeyed Christ's command, and on the Day of Pentecost, they received the promised power.

Today, we must do the same. If we expect to succeed in the work, we cannot ignore this first crucial element of Jesus' missions strategy. Like Jesus and those first Christians, we must "receive power when the Holy Spirit comes on [us]" (1:8).

This empowering is not only for church leaders; it is for every follower of Christ. The Bible says that on the Day of Pentecost, "they were *all* filled with the Holy Spirit" (2:4). Every believer must be empowered by the Holy Spirit because every believer has been commissioned as Christ's witness.

Witness. The second leg of the New Testament Strategy of the Spirit is witness. Jesus told His disciples, "You will be my witnesses...to the ends of the earth" (1:8). The Book of Acts is the true story of how the Early Church fulfilled that mandate.

In Acts, their witness included two elements, a clear presentation of the gospel and a demonstration of kingdom power. Today, our witness must include those same two elements. We must boldly proclaim Christ to all, and we must trust Him to confirm His word with signs following.

Mobilization. Finally, the New Testament Strategy of the Spirit includes mobilization. This is what we see happening in the Book of Acts. In Ephesus, Paul prayed with the twelve disciples to be empowered by the Spirit. Then, after he had trained them in the lecture hall of Tyrannus, he sent them out to evangelize Asia Minor (19:1-10).

Paul was simply following the example set by Jesus. Jesus trained His disciples, and He commanded them to wait in Jerusalem to be empowered by the Spirit. Finally, He sent them out to preach the good news and plant Spirit-empowered missionary churches.

We must do the same. If we will follow the New Testament Strategy of the Spirit, we, like the Early Church, will be successful in caring out the missionary mandate.

Today's Challenge

Today the church faces a great challenge. Throughout the world thousands of tribes and millions of people still wait to hear the good news for the first time. Some of those people may even live near you. Christ has commissioned us to take the good news to them. But, how can we accomplish such an enormous task?

The answer is that we can do it in Christ's strength. We can follow the example of the early disciples in Acts. They were convinced that, in the Spirit's power, they could do anything Christ had commanded.

The Book of Acts thus teaches us that the hope of reaching the nations does not lie in any humanly devised means. It lies, rather, in our determination to remain committed to Christ and His global mandate— and in our insistence that every believer be empowered by the Holy Spirit. We must therefore herald the final message of Jesus everywhere:

> *"But you will receive power*
> *when the Holy Spirit comes on you;*
> *and you will be my witnesses in Jerusalem,*
> *and in all Judea and Samaria,*
> *and to the ends of the earth"*
> ~ Acts 1:8 ~

Day 45: The Message of Acts

Other Works by Denzil R. Miller

Power Ministry: How to Minister in the Spirit's Power
(2004) (Also available in French, Portuguese,
Romanian, Malagasy, Kinyarwanda, and Chichewa)

*Empowered for Global Mission: A Missionary
Look at the Book of Acts* (2005)

From Azusa to Africa to the Nations (2005)
(Also available in French, Spanish, and Portuguese)

Acts: The Spirit of God in Mission (2007)

*In Step with the Spirit: Studies in the
Spirit-filled Walk* (2008)

*The Kingdom and the Power: The Kingdom of God:
A Pentecostal Interpretation* (2009)

*Experiencing the Spirit: A Study of the Work of
the Spirit in the Life of the Believer* (2009)

Teaching in the Spirit (2009)

*Power Encounter: Ministering in the Power and
Anointing of the Holy Spirit: Revised* (2009)
(Also available in French, Portuguese, Romanian,
Kiswahili and Chichewa)

*You Can Minister in God's Power: A Guide for
Spirit-filled Disciples* (2009)

*Proclaiming Pentecost: 100 Sermon Outlines on the
Power of the Holy Spirit* (2011) Associate editor with Mark
Turney, editor (Also available in French, Spanish,
Portuguese, Moore, Amharic, and Swahili)

Other Works By Denzil R. Miller

Globalizing Pentecostal Missions in Africa (2011)
Editor, with Enson Lwesya
(Also available in French, 2014)

The Spirit of God in Mission: A Vocational Commentary on the Book of Acts (2013)

The 1:8 Promise of Jesus: The Key to World Harvest (2012)

Power for Mission: The Africa Assemblies of God Mobilizing the Reach the Nations (2014)
Editor, with Enson Lwesya

Missionary Tongues Revisited: More than an Evidence: Revisiting Luke's Missional Perspective on Speaking in Tongues (2014)

These books can be purchased on the author's website:
www.DenzilRMiller.com

www.ingramcontent.com/pod-product-compliance
Lightning Source LLC
Chambersburg PA
CBHW061635040426
42446CB00010B/1434